THE LIBRARY
ST. MARY'S COLLEGE OF MARYLAND
ST. MARY'S CITY, MARYLAND 20686

76473

# OSCAR WILDE

BY THE SAME AUTHOR

BOHEMIA IN LONDON (Sketches and Essays), 1907.
A HISTORY OF STORY-TELLING, 1909.
EDGAR ALLAN POE, 1910.
THE HOOFMARKS OF THE FAUN, 1911.
PORTRAITS AND SPECULATIONS, 1913.

# OSCAR WILDE
## A CRITICAL STUDY

BY

ARTHUR RANSOME

THIRD EDITION

HASKELL HOUSE PUBLISHERS LTD.
*Publishers of Scarce Scholarly Books*
NEW YORK, N. Y. 10012
1971

First Published 1912

**HASKELL HOUSE PUBLISHERS LTD.**
*Publishers of Scarce Scholarly Books*
280 LAFAYETTE STREET
NEW YORK, N. Y. 10012

Library of Congress Catalog Card Number: 79-151283

Standard Book Number 8383-1230-6

Printed in the United States of America

TO
ROBERT ROSS

# NOTE

I WISH to thank Mr. Robert Ross, Wilde's literary executor, who has helped me in every possible way, allowed me to read many of the letters that Wilde addressed to him, and given much time out of a very busy life to the verification, from documents in his possession, of the biographical facts included in my book. I wish to thank Mr. Walter Ledger for much interesting information, and for the sight of many rare editions of Wilde's books that made possible the correction of several bibliographical errors into which I had fallen. I wish to thank Mr. Martin Secker for putting at my disposal his collection of late nineteenth-century literature. I wish to thank an anonymous author for lending me the proof-sheets of a forthcoming book, which will contain a full and accurate account of the legal proceedings for and against Wilde. Many of those who knew Wilde have helped me, by letter or in conversation, with valuable reminiscence. I would thank particularly M. Paul Fort, M. Remy de Gourmont, M. Stuart Merrill, and Mr. Reginald Turner.

The texts of Wilde's books that I have used throughout are these: Messrs. Methuen's limited edition of the works, and the five shilling edition issued by the same firm; Mr. Charles Carrington's

## NOTE

edition of *The Picture of Dorian Gray*; Mr. A. L. Humphrey's edition of *The Soul of Man under Socialism*; Mr. David Nutt's edition of *The Happy Prince and other Tales*. To these, as to the best, and in some cases the only, editions easily accessible, I must refer my readers. Much accurate observation is to be found in M. André Gide's "Oscar Wilde," published by the Mercure de France, and the result of much laborious and useful research is embodied in Mr. Stuart Mason's "Bibliography of the Poems of Oscar Wilde," published by Mr. Grant Richards.

## NOTE TO SECOND EDITION

The publication of this book in 1912 was the subject of a libel action which was brought against me in the King's Bench Division of the High Court of Justice, and was heard before Mr. Justice Darling and a Special Jury on four days in April 1913. In that action a verdict was given in my favour. In bringing out this new edition I have considered the question of reprinting the book in its original form, as I have a perfect right to do, but as I do not consider that the passages complained of are essential to the critical purpose of my book I have decided, in order to spare the feelings of those who might be pained by the further publication of those passages, to omit them from this edition.

ARTHUR RANSOME.

*May* 1913.

# CONTENTS

|  | PAGE |
|---|---|
| INTRODUCTORY | 9 |
| BIOGRAPHICAL SUMMARY | 24 |
| POEMS | 34 |
| ÆSTHETICISM | 61 |
| MISCELLANEOUS PROSE | 85 |
| INTENTIONS | 111 |
| THE THEATRE | 140 |
| DISASTER | 166 |
| DE PROFUNDIS | 171 |
| 1897–1900 | 194 |
| AFTERTHOUGHT | 220 |

# OSCAR WILDE

## I
## INTRODUCTORY

GILBERT, in 'The Critic as Artist,' complains that "we are overrun by a set of people who, when poet or painter passes away, arrive at the house along with the undertaker, and forget that their one duty is to behave as mutes. But we won't talk about them," he continues. "They are the mere body-snatchers of literature. The dust is given to one and the ashes to another, but the soul is out of their reach." That is not a warning lightly to be disregarded. No stirring up of dust and ashes is excusable, and none but brutish minds delight in mud-pies mixed with blood. I had no body-snatching ambition. Impatient of such criticism of Wilde as saw a law-court in *A House of Pomegranates*, and heard the clink of handcuffs in the flowing music of

*Intentions*, I wished, at first, to write a book on Wilde's work in which no mention of the man or his tragedy should have a place. I remembered that he thought Wainewright, the poisoner and essayist, too lately dead[1] to be treated in "that fine spirit of disinterested curiosity to which we owe so many charming studies of the great criminals of the Italian Renaissance." To-day it is Wilde who is too near us to be seen without a blurring of perspectives. Some day it will be possible to write of him with the ecstatic acquiescence that Nietzsche calls *Amor Fati*, as we write of Cæsar Borgia sinning in purple, Cleopatra sinning in gold, and Roberto Greene hastening his end by drab iniquity and grey repentance. But not yet. He only died a dozen years ago. I planned an artificial ignorance that should throw him to a distance where his books alone would represent him.

I was wrong, of course. Such wilful evasion would have been foolish in a contemporary critic of Shelley, worse than foolish in a critic of Wilde. An artist is unable to do everything for us. He gives us his work as a locked casket. Sometimes the wards

[1] He died in 1852. Wilde wrote in 1888.

are very simple and all the world have keys to fit; sometimes they are intricate and subtle, and the casket is only to be opened by a few, though all may taste imperfectly the precious essences distilling through the hinges. Sometimes, when our knowledge of an artist and of the conditions under which he wrote have been entirely forgotten, there are no keys, and the work of art remains a closed casket, like much early poetry, of which we can only say that it is cunningly made and that it has a secret. Why do we try to pierce the obscurity that surrounds the life of Shakespeare if not because an intenser (I might say a more accurate) enjoyment of his writings may be given us by a fuller knowledge of the existence out of which he wrote? It is for this that we study the Elizabethan theatre, and print upon our minds a picture of the projecting stage, the gallants smoking pipes and straddling their stools, the flag waving from above the tiled roof. We would understand his technique, but, still more, while we lack directer evidence, we would use these hints about the furniture of his mind's eye in moments of composition. Writers of Wordsworth's generation realized, at least subconsciously, that a work of art is not independent of knowledge. They tried to help us by printing at the head of a poem information about the circumstances of its conception. When a poet tells us that a sonnet was composed "on Westminster Bridge," or "suggested by Mr. Westell's views of the caves, etc., in Yorkshire," he is trying to ease for us the task of æsthetic reproduction to which his poem is a stimulus. There is a crudity about such obvious assistance, and it would be quite insufficient without the knowledge on which we draw unconsciously as we read. But the crudity of those pitiable little scraps of proffered information is not so remarkable as that of the presumptuous attempt to read a book as if it had fallen like manna from heaven, and that of the gross dullness of perception that can allow a man to demand of a poem or a picture that it shall itself compel him fully to understand it. To gain the privilege of a just appreciation of a man's books (if, indeed, such an appreciation is possible) we must know what place they took in his life, and handle the rough material that dictated even their most ethereal tissue. In the case of such a writer as Wilde, whose books are the by-products of a life more important than they in his own eyes, it is not only legitimate but necessary for understanding to look at books and life together as at a portrait of an artist by himself, and to read, as well as we may, between the touches of the brush. It is not that there is profit in trying to turn works of art into biographical data, though that may be a fascinating pastime. It is that biographical data cannot do other than assist us in our understanding of the works of art.

In any case, leaving on one side this question, admittedly subject to debate, it would have been ridiculous to study the writings alone of a man who said, not without truth, that he put his genius into his life, keeping only his talent for his books. I therefore changed my original intention, and, while concerned throughout with Wilde as artist and critic rather than as criminal, read his biographers and talked with his friends that I might be so far from forgetting as continually to perceive behind the books the spectacle of the man, vividly living his life and filling it as completely as he filled his works with his strange and brilliant personality.

It is too easy to talk glibly of the choice

between life and literature. No choice can be made between them. The whole is greater than its part, and literature is at once the child and the stimulus of life, inseparable from it. But, beside art, life has other activities, all of which aspire to the self-consciousness that art makes possible. The artist himself, for all his gift of tongues, is not blinded by the descending light to the plastic qualities of the existence that fires his words and is itself intensified by his speech. He, too, moves in walled town or on the green earth, and has a little time in which to build two memories, one for his fellows, and another, a secret diary, to carry with him when he dies. In his life, his books or pictures or brave harmonies of music are but moments, notes of colour in a composition vital to himself. And when we speak so carelessly of a choice between life and literature, we do not mean a choice. We only compare the vividness of a man's whole life, as we perceive it, with that of those portions of it that he spent in books. Sometimes we wonder which is more alive. In Wilde's case we compare a row of volumes, themselves remarkable, with a life that was the occupation of an agile and vivid personality for which a cloistered converse with itself was not enough, a personality that loved the lights and the bustle, the eyes and ears of the world, and the applause that does not have to wait for print.

Wilde was a kind of Wainewright, to whom his own life was very important. He saw art as self-expression and life as self-development. He felt that his life was material on which to practise his powers of creation, and handled it and brooded over it like a sculptor planning to make a dancing figure out of a pellet of clay. Even after its catastrophe he was still able to speak of his life as of a work of art, as if he had seen it from outside. Indeed, to a surprising extent, he had been a spectator of his own tragedy. In building his life his strong sense of the picturesque was not without admirable material, and he was able to face the street with a decorative and entertaining façade, which, unlike those of the palaces in Genoa, was not contradicted by dullness within. He made men see him as something of a dandy among authors, an amateur of letters in contrast with the professional maker of books and plays. If he wrote books he did not allow people to presume upon the fact, but retained the status of a gentleman. At the Court of Queen Joan of Naples he would have been a rival to Boccaccio, himself an adventurer. At the Court of James he would have crossed "Characters" with Sir Thomas Overbury. In an earlier reign he would have corresponded in sonnets with Sir Philip Sidney, played with Euphuism, been very kind to Jonson at the presentation of a masque, and never set foot in The Mermaid. Later, Anthony Hamilton might have been his friend, or with the Earl of Rochester he might have walked up Long Acre to belabour the watch without dirtying the fine lace of his sleeves. In no age would he have been a writer of the study. He talked, and wrote only to show that he could write. His writings are mostly vindications of the belief he had in them while still unwritten. It pleased him to pretend that his plays were written for wagers.

After making imaginary backgrounds for him, let us give him his own. This man, who would perhaps have found a perfect setting for himself in the Italy of the

## INTRODUCTORY

Renaissance, was born in 1854. Leigh Hunt, De Quincey, and Macaulay were alive. Wordsworth had only been dead four years. Tennyson was writing "Maud" and "The Idylls of the King." Borrow was wandering in wild Wales and finishing "The Romany Rye." Browning was preparing "Men and Women" for the press. Dickens was the novelist of the day, and had half a dozen books yet to write. Thackeray was busy on "The Newcomes." Matthew Arnold was publishing his "Poems." FitzGerald was working underground in the mine from which he was to extract the roses of Omar. Ruskin had just published "Stones of Venice," was arranging to buy the work of a young man called Rossetti, helping with the Working Men's College, and writing a pamphlet on the Crystal Palace. William Morris, younger even than Rossetti, was an undergraduate at Oxford, rhyming nightly, and exclaiming that, if this was poetry, it was very easy.

It is characteristic of great men that, born out of their time, they should come to represent it. Victor Hugo, in 1830, was a young man irreverently trying to overturn established tradition. He had to pack a theatre with his friends to save his play from being hissed. Now, looking back on that time, his enemies seem to have faded away, tired ghosts, and he to be alone upon the stage laying about him on backs of air. So far was the Elizabethan age from a true appreciation of Shakespeare that Webster could patronize him with praise of "his happy and copious industry." Shakespeare was a busy little dramatist, working away on the fringe of the great light cast by the effulgent majesty of Elizabeth. To-day Shakespeare divides with his queen the honour of naming the years they lived in. The nineties, the early nineties when Wilde's talent was in full fruition, seem now, at least in literature, to be coloured by the personality of Wilde and the movement foolishly called Decadent. But in the nineties, when Wilde was writing, he had a very few silent friends and a very great number of vociferous enemies. His books were laughed at, his poetry parodied, his person not kindly caricatured, and, even when his plays won popular applause, this hostility against him was only smothered, not choked. His disaster ungagged it, and few men have been sent to perdition with a louder cry of hounds behind them.

There was relief as well as hostility in the cry. Wilde had meant a foreign ideal, and one not too easy to follow. If he were right, then his detractors were wrong, and there was joy in the voices of those who taunted, pointing to the Old Bailey, "that is where the artistic life leads a man." There was also shown a curious inability to distinguish between the destruction of a man's body and the extinction of his mind's produce. When Wilde was sent to prison the spokesmen of the nineties were pleased to shout, "We have heard the last of him." To make sure of that they should have used the fires of Savonarola as well as the cell of Raleigh. They should have burnt his books as well as shutting up the writer. That sentence, so frequently iterated, that "No more would be heard of him," showed a remarkable error in valuation of his powers.

There was surprise in England when *Salomé* was played in Paris while its author was in prison. It seemed impossible that a man who had been sent to gaol for such offences as his could be an artist honoured out of his own country. Only after his death, upon the appearance of *De Profundis*, and translations of his writings into French, German, Italian, Spanish, Swedish, Yiddish, Polish, and Russian, did popular opinion recognize (if it has yet recognized) that the Old Bailey, the public disgrace and the imprisonment were only circumstances in Wilde's private tragedy that would have been terrible even without them, and that they were no guarantee of the worthlessness of what he wrote.

So far were Wilde's name and influence from ending with his personal disaster that they are daily gathering weight. Whether his writings are perfectly successful or not, they altered in some degree the course of literature in his time, and are still an active power when the wind has long blown away the dust of newspaper criticism with which they were received. It is already clear that Wilde has an historical importance too easily underestimated. His indirect influence is incalculable, for his attitude in writing gave literature new standards of valuation, and men are writing under their influence who would indignantly deny that their work was in any way dictated by Wilde.

A personality as vivid as his, exercised at once through books and in direct but perhaps less intimate social intercourse, cannot suddenly be wiped away like a picture on a slate. No man's life was crossed by Wilde's without experiencing a change. Men lived more vividly in his presence, and talked better than themselves. No common man lives and dies without altering, to some extent, the life about him and so the history of the world. How much wider is their influence who live their lives like flames, hurrying to death through their own enjoyment and expenditure alike of their bodies and their brains. " Pard-like spirits, beautiful and swift" are sufficiently rare and notable to be ensured against oblivion.

His personality was stronger than his will. When, as he often did, he set himself to imitation, he could not prevent himself from leaving his mark upon the counterfeit. He stole freely, but often mounted other men's jewels so well that they are better in his work than in their own. It is impossible to dismiss even his early poetry as without significance.  He left no form of literature exactly as he found it.  He brought back to the English stage a spirit of comedy that had been for many years in mourning.  He wrote a romantic play which necessitated a new manner of production, and may be considered the starting-point of the revolution in stage-management that, happily, is still proceeding.  He showed both in practice and theory the possibilities of creation open to the critic.  He found a new use for dialogue, and brought to England a new variety of the novel.  His work continually upset accepted canons and received views.  It placed, for example, the apparently settled question of sincerity in a new obscurity, and the distinction between decoration and realism in a new light.  One of the tests of novelty and beauty is that they should be a little out at elbows in an old æsthetic.  Wilde sets the subtlest problems before us, and I shall not be wasting time in posing them and showing that his work has at least this quality of what is beautiful and new, that it is impossible to apply to it definitions that were sufficient before it.  It will be necessary in considering his writing, as I hope to do, to digress again and again from book, or play, or poem into the abstract regions of speculation. Only so will it be possible to appreciate this man whose name was to have disappeared in 1895, whose work is likely to preserve that name long after oblivion has swallowed the well-intentioned prophets of its extinction.

Even so, however carefully I may discuss alike his work and the abstract and technical questions that it raises; however carefully I may gather evidence of his overflowing richness of personality, I shall not be able to make a complete and worthy portrait of the man. There are people, mostly of the generation before my own (though the youngest of us may come to it), who make a practice of suggesting our entire ignorance of a subject by demanding that we shall define it in a few words. "Say what you think of him in a sentence." If I could do that, do you think I should be going to the labour of writing a book? One cannot define in a sentence a man whom it has taken God several millions of years to make. In a dozen chapters it is no less impossible. The utmost one can do, and that only with due humility, is to make an essay in definition.

## II

## BIOGRAPHICAL SUMMARY

"THE necessity of complying with times, and of sparing persons, is the great impediment of biography. History may be formed from permanent monuments and records; but Lives can only be written from personal knowledge, which is growing every day less, and in a short time is lost for ever. What is known can seldom be immediately told; and when it might be told, it is no longer known. The delicate features of the mind, the nice discriminations of character, and the minute peculiarities of conduct, are soon obliterated; and it is surely better that caprice, obstinacy, frolic, and folly, however they might delight in the description, should be silently forgotten, than that, by wanton merriment and unseasonable detection, a pang should be given to a widow, a daughter, a brother, or a friend. As the process of these narratives is now bringing me among my contemporaries, I begin to feel myself *walking upon ashes under which the fire is not extinguished,* and coming to the time of which it will be proper rather to say *nothing that is false, than all that is true*" (Samuel Johnson, in his "Life of Addison").

BEFORE proceeding to the main business of the book, an examination of Wilde's work, I wish to set before myself and my readers a summary biography which may hereafter be useful for our reference. Much of the life of Wilde is so bound up with his work as to be incapable of separate treatment; but, on the other hand, dates clog a page, and facts do not always enjoy their just value when dovetailed into criticism. In this chapter I shall set down the facts of Wilde's parentage and education, up to the time when it becomes possible and advisable to speak of his life and his work together. Thenceforward, I shall do little more than note the dates of events and publications (reserving to myself the right of repeating them when I find it convenient), and make, as it were, a skeleton that shall gather flesh from the ensuing pages of the book.

Oscar Fingal O'Flahertie Wills Wilde was born on October 16, 1854, at 21, Westland Row, Dublin. His father was William Wilde, knighted in 1864, a celebrated oculist and aurist, a man of great intellectual activity and uncertain temper, a runner after girls, with a lusty enjoyment of life, and a delight in falling stars and thunderstorms. His mother, whose maiden name was Elgee, was a clever woman, who, when very young, writing as "Speranza" in a revolutionary paper, had tried to rouse Irishmen to the storming of Dublin Castle. She read Latin and Greek, but was ready to suffer fools for the sake of social adulation. She was clever enough to enjoy astonishing the *bourgeois*, but her cleverness seldom carried her further. When Wilde was born, she was twenty-eight and her husband thirty-nine. They were people of consideration in Dublin. His schoolfellows did not have to ask Wilde who his father was. It is said, that before Wilde's birth, his mother had hoped for a girl. He was a second son. His elder brother, William, became a journalist in London, and died in 1899. He had a sister, Isola, younger than himself, who died in childhood. Her death suggested the poem 'Requiescat.' To

## BIOGRAPHICAL SUMMARY 27

him, as to De Quincey, a sister brought the idea of mortality. There are exceptions to that fine rule of Hazlitt's brother: "No young man believes he shall ever die." De Quincey looking across his sister's death-bed through an open window on a summer day, and Wilde, thinking of

> "All her bright golden hair
> Tarnished with rust,
> She that was young and fair
> Fallen to dust,"

felt the fingers of death before their time. Like most of Wilde's early melodies, his lament is sung to a borrowed lyre, but the thing is so sweet that it seems ungracious to remember its indebtedness to Hood.[1]

Both Sir William and Lady Wilde busied themselves in collecting folk-lore. Wilde in boyhood travelled with his father to visit ruins and gather superstitions. His childhood must have had a plentiful mythology. Wilde and his brother were not excluded from the extravagant conversations of their mother's

---

[1] "Take her up tenderly,
Lift her with care;
Fashioned so slenderly,
Young, and so fair!"

*salon.* Any precocity they showed was encouraged, if only by that curious atmosphere of agile cleverness. There are no valuable anecdotes of his childhood, but it is said that his mother always thought that Oscar was less brilliant than her elder son.

When he was nine he was sent to the Portora Royal School at Enniskillen, where he behaved well, did not particularly distinguish himself, did not play games, read a great deal, and was very bad at mathematics. In the holidays he travelled with his mother in France. Leaving Portora in 1871, he went with an exhibition to Trinity College, Dublin, where he was elected to a Queen's Scholarship.

In 1874, he won the Berkeley Gold Medal for Greek. In the same year he left Dublin for Oxford, taking a scholarship and matriculating at Magdalen. In 1876 he took a First Class in Classical Moderations, always a sufficient proof of sound learning, and, in 1878, he took a First Class in Literae Humaniores. In 1877 he travelled in Italy and went to Greece with Professor Mahaffy. This experience had great influence on his attitude towards art, filled the classical dic-

## BIOGRAPHICAL SUMMARY 29

tionary with life, and made the figures of mythology so luminous that he was tempted to overwork them. In 1878 he read the Newdigate Prize Poem in the Sheldonian Theatre.

On leaving Oxford he brought to London a small income, a determination to conquer the town, and a reputation as a talker. He took rooms in the Adelphi. He adopted a fantastic costume to emphasise his personality, and, perhaps to excuse it, spoke of the ugliness of modern dress. In three years he had won the recognition of Punch, which, thenceforward, caricatured him several times a month.

In 1881 he published his first book, a volume of poems, discussed in the next chapter. Five editions of it were immediately sold. His costume and identification with the æsthetic movement of that time determined his selection as a lecturer in America. The promoters of his tour there were, however, anxious to help not the æsthetic movement but the success of a play that laughed at it. He went to America in 1882, and again in 1883, on the latter occasion to see the production of *Vera*. On his return from the first visit he went to Paris, where he finished *The Duchess of Padua*, which was not published till 1908. In 1891 it was produced in New York, when twenty copies were printed for the actors and for private circulation. It is likely that in 1883, while in Paris, he began *The Sphinx*, upon which he worked at various periods before its publication in 1894.

Returning to England, he took rooms in Charles Street, Haymarket, and lectured in the provinces. In 1884 he married Constance Mary Lloyd, who brought him enough money to enable him to take No. 16 Tite Street, Chelsea, which was his home until 1895. He wrote for a number of periodical newspapers, and, for two years, edited The Woman's World.

In 1885 'The Truth of Masks' appeared as 'Shakespeare and Stage Costume' in The Nineteenth Century. In 1886 he began that course of conduct that was to lead to his downfall in 1895. In 1887 he published 'Lord Arthur Savile's Crime,' 'The Canterville Ghost,' 'The Sphinx without a Secret,' and 'The Model Millionaire,' which were issued together in 1891. In 1888 he published *The Happy Prince and other Tales*. In 1889

'The Portrait of Mr. W. H.' appeared in Blackwood's Magazine. 'Pen, Pencil and Poison' appeared in the Fortnightly Review in 1889, 'The Decay of Lying' in the Nineteenth Century in the same year, and 'The Critic as Artist' in the Nineteenth Century in 1890. *A House of Pomegranates* and *Intentions,* in which these three essays were reprinted with 'The Truth of Masks,' were published in 1891. In the same year 'The Soul of Man under Socialism' appeared in the Fortnightly Review. *The Picture of Dorian Gray* appeared in Lippincott's Magazine in 1890. The Preface was published separately in the Fortnightly Review in 1891. He added several chapters, and *The Picture of Dorian Gray* was published in book form in 1891. Much of his time was spent in Paris, and there, before the end of the year, he wrote *Salomé*. In 1892 that play was prohibited by the Censor when Madame Sarah Bernhardt had begun to rehearse it for production at the Palace Theatre. It was first produced in Paris, at the Théâtre de L'Œuvre, in 1896. *Lady Windermere's Fan* was produced on February 20, 1892, by Mr. George Alexander at the St. James's Theatre.

*A Woman of No Importance* was produced on April 19, 1893, by Mr. H. Beerbohm Tree at the Haymarket Theatre, where, on January 3, 1895, he produced *An Ideal Husband*. On February 14, 1895, Mr. George Alexander produced *The Importance of Being Earnest* at the St. James's.

With the production of these plays Wilde became not only a caricatured celebrity but a popular success. He lived extravagantly. In 1895 the applause was turned to execration, when he lost in a prosecution for criminal libel that he brought against the Marquis of Queensberry, and was himself arrested on a more serious charge. The jury disagreed, and he was released on bail, perhaps in the hope that he would leave the country. He waited the re-trial, was convicted, and sentenced to two years' imprisonment with hard labour, which sentence he served. Towards the end of his time in prison he wrote the letter from which *De Profundis* (published in 1905) is extracted. After his release he went to Berneval-sur-mer, near Dieppe, where he began *The Ballad of Reading Gaol*, which he revised in Naples and Paris, and published pseudonymously in 1898. He also wrote

## BIOGRAPHICAL SUMMARY

two letters on prison abuses, which were published in the Daily Chronicle on May 28, 1897, and March 24, 1898. He lived in Italy, Switzerland and France. He died in Paris on November 30, 1900. He was buried on December 3 in the Bagneux Cemetery. On July 20, 1909, his remains were removed to Père Lachaise.

# III

## POEMS

It is a relief to turn from a list of bibliographical and biographical dates to the May-day colouring of a young man's first book; to forget for a moment the suffering that is nearly twenty years ahead, and to think of "undergraduate days at Oxford; days of lyrical ardour and of studious sonnet-writing; days when one loved the exquisite intricacy and musical repetitions of the ballade, and the villanelle with its linked long-drawn echoes and its curious completeness; days when one solemnly sought to discover the proper temper in which a triolet should be written; delightful days, in which, I am glad to say, there was far more rhyme than reason." It is too easy to forget this note in Wilde's personality, that he sounded again and again, and that was not cracked even by the terrible experiences whose symbol was imprisonment.

To the end of his life Wilde retained the enthusiasm, the power of self-abandon to a moment of emotion, the delight in difficult beauty, in accomplished loveliness, that made his Oxford years so happy a memory, and gave his first book a savour quite independent of its poetical value.

Ballade and villanelle, rondeau and triolet, the names of these French forms were enough to set the key for a young craftsman's reverie. But the university at that time was full of lively influences. Walter Pater's "Renaissance" had not long left the press. Its author, that grave man, was to be met in his panelled rooms, ready to advise, to point the way to rare books, and to talk of the secrets of his art. Pater in those days was a new classic, the private possession of those young men who found his books "the holy writ of beauty." The new classics of the generation before—Tennyson and Arnold and Browning—had not yet faded into that false antiquity that follows swift upon the heels of popular recognition. The scholar gipsy had not long been given his place in the mythology of "Oxford riders blithe," and the trees in Bagley Wood were still a little tremulous at his presence.

Browning's "The Ring and the Book" had been published ten years before. Queen Victoria's approval of Tennyson may have somewhat marred him in the eyes of youthful seekers after subtlety, but the early poems offered a pleasant opportunity for discriminating appreciation. It was not very long since Swinburne "had set his age on fire by a volume of very perfect and very poisonous poetry." Morris, the first edition of whose "Defence of Guenevere," though published in 1857, was not exhausted till thirteen years later, was a master not yet so widely admired as to deny to his disciples the delight of a personal and almost daring loyalty. Rossetti's was a still more powerful influence.

All these factors must be remembered in any attempt to reconstruct the atmosphere in which Wilde wrote his early poems. Nor must we forget that when Wilde entered that atmosphere as an undergraduate he had an unusual training behind him. He had known another university, and carried away from it a gold medal for Greek. He was an Irishman whose nationality had been momentarily intensified by his revolutionary mother and his own name. And, perhaps still more important, he was a very youthful cosmopolitan, had been often abroad, knew a good deal of French poetry, and had been able to date one of his earliest poems from that light-hearted Avignon where the Popes once held their court, and whence the dancing on the broken bridge has sent a merry song throughout the world.

It is curious to see this young lover of Théophile Gautier and old intricate rhyme-forms, winning the Newdigate Prize for a poem in decasyllabic couplets on a set subject. Many bad and a few good poets have won that prize, and it constitutes, I suppose, a sort of academic recognition that a man writes verse. Wilde was always pleased with recognition, of whatever quality, and was, perhaps, induced to compete on finding himself curiously favoured by the subject chosen for the year, which happened to be *Ravenna*. He had visited Ravenna on his way to Greece in the previous long vacation, and so was equipped with memories denied to his rivals. He saw the city "across the sedge and mire," when they could only see her on the map. He knew "the lonely pillar, rising on the plain" where Gaston de Foix had died. And, in Italian woods, he had actually watched, hoping to see and hear

> "Some goat-foot Pan make merry minstrelsy
> Amid the reeds! some startled Dryad-maid
> In girlish flight! or lurking in the glade,
> The soft brown limbs, the wanton treacherous face
> Of woodland god!"

The wordy piece of rhetoric that was published after winning him the prize is enriched by some pictorial effects that are almost effects of poetry. But the best that can or need be said of the whole is, that it is an admirable prize poem.

Three years later he published his first book.

*Poems*, bound in white vellum, decorated with gold, and beautifully printed, contains work done before and after *Ravenna*. The most obvious quality of this work, and that which is most easily and most often emphasized, is its richness in imitations. But there is more in it than that. It is full of variations on other men's music, but they are variations to which the personality of the virtuoso has given a certain uniformity. Wilde played the sedulous ape with sufficient self-consciousness and sufficient failure to show that he might himself be somebody. His emulative practice of his art asks for a closer consideration than that usually given to it. Let me borrow an admirable phrase from M. Remy de Gourmont, and say that a "dissociation of ideas" is necessary in thinking of imitation. To describe a young poet's work as derivative is not the same thing as to condemn it. All work is derivative more or less, and to pour indiscriminate contempt on Wilde's imitations because they are imitations, is to betray a lamentable ignorance of the history of poetry. There is no need too seriously to defend this early work. Wilde's reputation can stand without or even in spite of it. But it is worth while to notice that the worst it suggests is that young poets should be very careful to be bad critics, since they always do ill if they imitate the best contemporary models. They do better to copy poetasters, whom they must believe to be Miltons. When Coleridge admires Bowles, makes forty transcriptions from his poems for distribution among his friends, and imitates him as wholeheartedly as he can, he will but gain in comparison with his original. There is nothing in the master strong enough to impose itself upon the pupil. When Keats, full of admiration, imitates Leigh Hunt, he is not very heavily impeded in his search for Keats. But when Wilde blows the horn of Morris, an echo from that Norseman's lungs throws out of harmony the notes of his disciple. When he touches Rossetti's lute his melody is blurred by the thrum of the strings that the Italian's fingers have so lately left. In fifty years' time it will, perhaps, be safe to imitate Swinburne. It is not so at present.

Even in springing from the ground of prose into the air of song, it is wise to choose ground that age has worn or that is not itself remarkable. When Coleridge reads Purchas—

"In Xamdu did Cublai Can build a stately Palace encompassing sixteen miles of plain ground with a wall, wherein are fertile Meddowes, pleasant Springs, delightfull Streames, and all sorts of beasts of chase and game, and in the middest thereof a sumptuous house of pleasure"——

and rewrites it—

"In Xanadu did Kubla Khan
A stately pleasure dome decree:
Where Alph the sacred river ran
Through caverns measureless to man
Down to a sunless sea.

> So twice five miles of fertile ground
> With walls and towers were girdled round:
> And there were gardens bright with sinuous rills
> Where blossomed many an incense-bearing tree;
> And here were forests ancient as the hills,
> Enfolding sunny spots of greenery"——

he works a true magic, bringing two out of one, and setting beside Purchas something that we can independently enjoy. Purchas died so long ago. He and Coleridge have different worlds behind them. But when Wilde remembers a passage in his favourite book, written not a dozen years before, and asks why he should not make personal to himself the description of the manifold life of Mona Lisa, that ends, "all this has been to her but as the sound of lyres and flutes"; when he prefixes two verses of explanation to a rhymed elaboration of that sentence—

> "But all this crowded life has been to thee
>   No more than lyre, or lute, or subtle spell
> Of viols, or the music of the sea
>   That sleeps, a mimic echo, in the shell"——

he only puts it out of drawing. It is impossible to avoid a comparison, because Pater and Wilde are so close together, alike in time and feeling.

'Eleutheria,' a section at the beginning of the book, includes a number of discreet sacrifices on the altar of Milton. Here Wilde does much better. Some of these exercises, which are among the most interesting he wrote, suggest a new view of the morale of imitation. With Wilde in this mood, imitation (to use one of those renewals of popular sayings that were the playthings of his mind), was the sincerest form of parody. Now parody is a branch of criticism. The critics of the music-hall stage are those favourite comedians who imitate their fellow-actors. Lewis Carroll is a negligible critic neither of Longfellow nor of Tennyson. Parody's criticism is too often facile, seeking applause by the readiest means, holding up to ridicule rather than to examination faults rather than excellences, exaggerating tricks of manner and concerning itself not all with personality. Wilde's parodies are at once more valuable and more sincere. He tries to catch not only the letter but the spirit, and does indeed present a clearer view of Milton than is contained in many academic essays. An accusation of mere plagiary is made impossible by his openness. He writes a sonnet on Milton, a sonnet on Louis Napoleon, and then, matching even the title of his model, a sonnet on the Massacre of the Christians in Bulgaria. Let me print the sonnet "On the Late Massacre in Piedmont":—

> "Avenge, O Lord, thy slaughter'd saints whose bones
> Lie scatter'd on the Alpine mountains cold;
> Ev'n them who kept thy truth so pure of old,
> When all our fathers worshipped stocks and stones,
> Forget not: in thy book record their groans
> Who were thy sheep, and in their ancient fold
> Slain by the bloody Piedmontese that roll'd
> Mother with infant down the rocks. Their moans
> The vales redoubled to the hills, and they
> To Heav'n. Their martyr'd blood and ashes sow
> O'er all the Italian fields, where still doth sway
> The triple tyrant; that from these may grow
> An hundredfold, who having learned thy way
> Early may fly the Babylonian woe."

And then Wilde's:—

> "Christ, dost thou live indeed? or are thy bones
> Still straitened in their rock-hewn sepulchre?
> And was thy Rising only dreamed by Her
> Whose love of thee for all her sin atones?
> For here the air is horrid with men's groans,
> The priests who call upon thy name are slain,
> Dost thou not hear the bitter wail of pain
> From those whose children lie upon the stones?

> Come down, O Son of God! incestuous gloom
> Curtains the land, and through the starless night
> Over thy Cross a Crescent moon I see!
> If thou in very truth didst burst the tomb
> Come down, O Son of Man! and show thy might,
> Lest Mahomet be crowned instead of Thee!"

This is a very different thing from the blind plagiary of those who cannot see their own way, and are themselves surprised to find that they have stolen. In their case, mistrust of their own powers is justifiable. But here, when the young poet, as an exercise—indeed as more than an exercise—catches the accent of Milton in words that deliberately set the doubtful faith of our day beside the noble assurance of the Puritans, and show by implication what that absolute belief meant to Milton, we are in the presence not of flattery, but of criticism, of exact appreciation. On the next page is the sonnet 'Quantum Mutata,' with the lines:—

> "Witness the men of Piedmont, chiefest care
>  Of Cromwell, when with impotent despair
> The Pontiff in his painted portico
>  Trembled before our stern ambassadors";

and the suggestion, certainly not personal to

Wilde, but chosen for its fitness to the poet of whom he is thinking—

> "that luxury
> With barren merchandise piles up the gate
> Where noble thoughts and deeds should enter by:
> Else might we still be Milton's heritors."

If we were to take this view of the character of Wilde's imitations it would be an easy task to run through most of the book, showing how carefully he acknowledges his indebtedness to Arnold, to Swinburne, to Morris, much as a creative critic like Walter Pater courteously sets the name of Pico della Mirandola, or of Sir Thomas Browne, at the head of a piece of his own writing of which they have been less the occasion than the chosen keystone. But there is no need.

It is more important to the student of Wilde to notice that the book had a popular success, and a success in no way due to any praise from the contemporary critics who, naturally enough, were unable to consider *Poems* as the first book of a great man, could not review it in the light of his later writings, and attacked it whole-heartedly, perhaps because they were flattered by the ease with which they detected its openly-acknowledged borrowings. Five editions were sold immediately, and this not very trustworthy success increased or confirmed Wilde's confidence in himself. The readiness of the public to throw their opinion in the critics' teeth was partly due, I think, to precisely those qualities for which the book was attacked. Much of this unusual eagerness of ordinary people to buy poetry, a commodity that they seldom think worth money, may be attributed to the curiosity which Wilde had contrived to stimulate by carefully calculated eccentricity. But such curiosity would be more easily satisfied by the sight of the man than by the reading of his poems. It is hardly enough to explain the sale of five editions of a book of verse. I think we may look for another reason of the book's popularity in the fact that Wilde, so far from inventing a new poetry, happened to summarize in himself the poetry of his time. He made himself, as it were, the representative poet of his period, a middleman between the muses and the public. People who had heard of Rossetti and Swinburne, but never read them, were able to recover their self-respect by purchasing Wilde.

And this leads us back to the book. All the defects of this young man's verse became qualities that contributed to its popular success. It was imitative: it summed up a period of poetry. It was overweighted with allusion: nothing could be more poetical in the ears of readers not trained by an austere Bowyer to a distrust of Pierian springs, lutes, lyres, Pegasus, and Hippocrene.

"In fancy I can almost hear him now, exclaiming Harp? Harp? Lyre? Pen and ink, boy, you mean! Muse, boy, Muse. Your nurse's daughter, you mean! Pierian spring? Oh aye! the cloister pump, I suppose." (Coleridge on Bowyer, in the "Biographia Literaria.")

The presence in verse of certain names of places and persons has come to be taken as implicit evidence of poetry. Where Venus is, there must poetry be; Helicon, Narcissus, Endymion (after Keats), and a score of others have become a sort of poetical counters that careless eyes do not distinguish from the sterling coin. Wilde makes full use of them, and, perhaps, trusting to the capital letters to carry them through, frequently decorates his verse with names of similar character not yet so hackneyed as to be immediately recognized as poetry. This kind of allusion flatters the reader's learning. Sometimes he brings colour into his verse by the use of a reference that must be unintelligible to a large part of his audience, and seems quite irrelevant to those who take the trouble to follow it, and have not the good fortune to hit upon the correct clue. For example, in 'The New Helen':—

"Alas, alas, thou wilt not tarry here,
  But, like that bird, the servant of the sun,
    Who flies before the north wind and the night,
So wilt thou fly our evil land and drear,
  Back to the tower of thine old delight,
  And the red lips of young Euphorion."

Now that, though not poetry, is a pleasant piece of colour. But, leaving aside the question of the bird, the servant of the sun, itself not easy to resolve, young Euphorion, who has served Wilde's verse well enough in having scarlet lips, is more than a little puzzling. Wilde probably remembers Part II of Goethe's "Faust." Achilles and Helen are said, as ghosts, to have had a child called Euphorion, but Goethe makes him the son of Faust and Helen, named in the legend Justus Faust. He leaps from earth when " scarcely called to life," and "out of the deep" invites his mother to follow him not to any "tower of old delight," but to "the gloomy realm." The reference is wilful, but Euphorion is a wonderful name.

Sometimes, indeed, the verse gains nothing from such allusion. For example, in the same poem:—

"Nay, thou wert hidden in that hollow hill
  With one who is forgotten utterly,
    *That discrowned Queen men call the Erycine.*"

This is simply learning put in for its own sake by the young scholar delighting in his knowledge of antiquity. The line that I have printed in italics is no more than a riddle whose answer is Venus, sometimes called Erycina (Erycina ridens) because she had a temple on Mount Eryx. Wilde means that Helen was hidden with the spirit of beauty (Venus) now shamefully neglected. He delighted in such riddles and disguised references, and they certainly helped his less cultured readers to feel that in reading him they were intimate with more poetry than they had read. In 'The Burden of Itys,' to take a last example, he says, addressing the nightingale:—

> "Light-winged and bright-eyed miracle of the wood!
>   If ever thou didst soothe with melody
> One of that little clan, that brotherhood
>   Which loved the morning-star of Tuscany
> More than the perfect sun of Raphael
> And is immortal, sing to me! for I too love thee well."

Sir Piercie Shafton might choose such a method of referring to the Pre-Raphaelite Brotherhood. Indeed, so far does Wilde carry his ingenuity that we are reminded of the defects of that school of verse that Johnson called the metaphysical, whose virtues are too generally forgotten. He hears the wind in the trees as Palæstrina playing the organ in Santa Maria on Easter Day. With half an echo of Browning he describes a pike as "some mitred old bishop *in partibus*," and, with a true seventeenth-century conceit, speaks of the early rose as "that sweet repentance of the thorny briar."

This ready-made or artificial poetry lacked, however, the firm intellectual substructure that could have infused into ornament and elaboration the vitalizing breath of unity. Wilde was uncertain of himself, and, in each one of the longer poems, rambled on, gathering flowers that would have seemed better worth having if he had not had so many of them. Doubtful of his aim in individual poems, he was doubtful of his inclinations as a poet. Nothing could more clearly illustrate this long wavering of his mind than a list of the poets whom he admired sufficiently to imitate. I have mentioned Morris, Swinburne, Arnold, and Rossetti; but these are not enough. In swift caprice he rifled a score of orchards. He very honestly confesses in 'Amor Intellectualis' that he had often "trod the vales of Castaly," sailed the sea "which the nine Muses hold in empery," and never turned home unladen.

> "Of which despoilèd treasures these remain,
>   Sordello's passion, and the honeyed line
> Of young Endymion, lordly Tamburlaine
>   Driving his pampered jades, and more than these
> The seven-fold vision of the Florentine,
>   And grave-browed Milton's solemn harmonies."

Milton, Dante, Marlowe, Keats and Browning, with those I have already named, and others, make up a goodly list of sufferers by this lighthearted corsair's piracies. He built with their help a brilliant coloured book, full of ingenuity, a boy's criticism of the objects of his admiration, almost a rhymed dictionary of mythology, whose incongruity is made apparent by those poems in which, leaving his classics passionately aside, he went, like a scholar gipsy, to seek a new accomplishment in the simplicity of folk-song.

Wilde's reputation as a poet does not rest on this first book, but on half a dozen poems that include 'The Harlot's House,' 'A Symphony in Yellow,' 'The Sphinx' and 'The Ballad of Reading Gaol,' and alone are worthy of a place beside his work in prose. But, though poetry is rare in it, it will presently be recognized that the first books of few men are so rich in autobiography. We have seen that the book is an index to his reading: let us see now how many indications it gives us of his life.

Threaded through the book, between the longer poems, runs an itinerary of his travels in Italy and Greece, written by a young man very conscious of being a poet, and keenly sensible of what it was fitting he should feel. In Italy, for example, he thought that he owed himself a conversion to the Catholic faith:—

> " Before yon field of trembling gold
>   Is garnered into dusty sheaves,
>   Or ere the autumn's scarlet leaves
> Flutter as birds adown the wold,

I may have run the glorious race,
 And caught the torch while yet aflame,
 And called upon the holy name
Of him who now doth hide his face."

He wrote almost as a Catholic might write, and spoke of the Pope as "the prisoned shepherd of the Church of God." But later, when

"The silver trumpets ran across the Dome:
 The people knelt upon the ground with awe:
 And borne upon the necks of men I saw,
Like some great God, the Holy Lord of Rome,"

he turned, as a puritan might have turned, from the emblem, triple-crowned, and clothed in red and white, of Christ's sovereignty, to remember a passage in the gospels: "Foxes have holes, and birds of the air have nests; but the Son of Man hath not where to lay his head."

He had a Calvinistic, half-shocked and half-exultant vision of his own iniquity, this undergraduate of twenty-three:—

"My heart is as some famine-murdered land
 Whence all good things have perished utterly,
 And well I know my soul in Hell must lie
If I this night before God's throne should stand."

Yet he took hope:—

> "My nets gaped wide with many a break and flaw,
>   Nathless I threw them as my final cast
>   Into the sea, and waited for the end.
> When lo! a sudden glory! and I saw
>   From the black waters of my tortured past
>   The argent splendour of white limbs ascend!"

He had, in short, a religious experience, such as is known by most young men. Perhaps it would be more accurate to say that he was disturbed, delightfully disturbed, by feeling that a religious experience was possible to him. He went on to Greece, and, remembering Plato, forgot the half-hoped, half-feared sensation of a wholly voluntary repose in Christianity.

He returned to Oxford, to win the Newdigate Prize in the next year, and to remember, with something of a girl's adventurous regret for a lover whom she has rejected, his Italian emotion. All this is written down in 'The Burden of Itys':—

> "This English Thames is holier far than Rome,
>   Those harebells like a sudden flush of sea
>   Breaking across the woodland, with the foam
>     Of meadow-sweet and white anemone

To fleck their blue waves,—God is likelier there
Than hidden in that crystal-hearted star the pale
monks bear";

and, in a later stanza :—

"strange, a year ago
I knelt before some crimson Cardinal
Who bare the Host across the Esquiline,
And now—those common poppies in the wheat seem
twice as fine."

'Panthea,' in language that suggests that he is looking for approval from the eyes of Swinburne, describes his substitute for that refused conversion. It is the creed of a young poet who finds the gods asleep, and does not care, because of Darwin, Evolution, and the Law of the Conservation of Energy.

"With beat of systole and of diastole
One grand great life throbs through earth's giant
heart,
And mighty waves of single Being roll
From nerveless germ to man, for we are part
Of every rock and bird and beast and hill,
One with the things that prey on us, and one with
what we kill."

And :—

"From lower cells of waking life we pass
To full perfection; thus the world grows old : "

and :—

> "This hot hard flame with which our bodies burn
> Will make some meadow blaze with daffodil,
> Ay! and those argent breasts of thine will turn
> To water-lilies; the brown fields men till
> Will be more fruitful for our love to-night,
> Nothing is lost in Nature, all things live in Death's despite."

It is boy's thought, as serious as the sentimental dreaming of a girl. There is no need to laugh at either. No young girl ever yet made a great poem out of her inexperience, nor has any young man turned to great art his hurried reading of the universe. But few great men have been without such thoughts in youth, and the noblest women can remember girlish dreams of an incredible unreality.

After taking his degree Wilde left Oxford and came to London to build up that phantom of himself that helped to advertize him, and, at the same time, to make his progress difficult. He dedicates a sonnet to 'My Friend Henry Irving,' another to Sarah Bernhardt, and two to Ellen Terry, 'Written at the Lyceum Theatre.' We have an impression of the young man, more elaborately dressed than he can afford, paying extravagant, delightful compliments, and quickly gaining the sort of reputation that was given to gallants of an older time, who knew actors, and had their seats on the stage.

Finally, and certainly most important in his own eyes, the book contains a record of the love affair which, in a sense, balanced the abortive religious experience. He fell in love with an actress, who found him quite delightful, did not love him, let him love her for a summer, and then told him not to waste his time. Wilde, as a young poet, probably came to town prepared to fall in love, just as he had gone to Italy prepared to be converted to Catholicism. His actress may have recognised that this was so, and been ready, within reason, to play the part assigned her. Through Wilde's magnificent phrasing there appears a replica of the love affairs of how many boys with women wiser than themselves and not without a sense of humour.

> "Ah! hadst thou liked me less and loved me more,
>   Through all these summer days of joy and rain,
> I had not now been sorrow's heritor,
>   Or stood a lackey in the House of Pain."

But he had not to grumble; he had been able

to love her learnedly in sonnets and gallantly in serenades. He had:—

"Stood face to face with Beauty, known indeed
  The Love which moves the Sun and all the Stars!"

That was really all that he had needed, but an awakening critical faculty told him that he won more pain than poetry.

"Had my lips been smitten into music by the kisses that
  but made them bleed,
You had walked with Bice and the angels on that
  verdant and enamelled mead."

He was disappointed, but the fault was not his, not his lady's, but due only to impatience. He who wills to love has rhetoric in his feeling, and, though he wrote—

"I have made my choice, have lived my poems, and,
  though youth is gone in wasted days,
I have found the lover's crown of myrtle better than
  the poet's crown of bays,"

we cannot help thinking that we know better.

The book is the monument of Wilde's boyhood, and contains its history. Perhaps that, though it may save it from oblivion, is the reason of its failure. It is too immediate an attempt to translate life into literature. Sometimes it even suggests that there has been an attempt to make life simply for the purpose of transcribing it. Wilde disguised it in elaboration, but it wears the mask with an ingenuous awkwardness. It is so youthful. Indeed, the youth of the book is its justification, and helps it to throw a flickering light upon his later work. For Wilde never entirely lost his boyhood, and died, as he had mostly lived, young. Five years after the publication of *Poems* he wrote a letter in which, catching exactly the mood of his undergraduate days of ten years before, he said that he wished he could grave his sonnets on an ivory tablet, since sonnets should always look well. That is the precise sentiment of those who seek "to discover the proper temper in which a triolet should be written." It was his whenever he wished. But, though he could recapture the mood, and assume again the attitude, he did not allow himself to imitate the work that mood and attitude had produced. In that white vellum volume were harvested all the wild oats of the intellect that he did not leave to later gleaners. He was free thenceforth, and seldom again, until the magnificent confession *De Profundis*, did he allow his experiences the use of the first person.[1] He had done with the crude subjectivity of boyhood, whose capital "I" seems so unreal beside the complete fusions of soul and body, manner and material, that Art demands and that he was later to achieve.

[1] Except, of course, in the lectures. We must remember their occasion, and that it never occurred to him to reprint them or count them among his works.

# IV

## ÆSTHETICISM

"I NEVER object," said Coleridge, "to a certain degree of disputatiousness in a young man from the age of seventeen to that of four or five and twenty, provided I find him always arguing on one side of the question." Coleridge would seem to reserve legitimate dispute for the very young, did we not remember that academic education began and ended earlier in his day. Boys went to college at seventeen. I do not think he would have objected to the disputatiousness of Wilde, although he was well over twenty-five before he left the noisy field of argument, if, indeed, he left it at all. Wilde, at least, would have pleased Coleridge by arguing always on one side of the question, though it is possible that Coleridge would not have recognized that that side was his own. At Oxford, Wilde had already begun to count himself, if not an inventor, at least an exponent of the æsthetic theories of life that were then disturbing with fitful movements the stagnant surface of British Philistinism. He did not plan a Pantisocracy, and would have turned with fright from Coleridge's sturdy proposal to harden the bodies of those accustomed to intellectual and sedentary labour until they were fitted to share in the tilling of the soil. But he was discontented with life as it was commonly lived, and had learnt to hope that it might be beautified by being set among beautiful things. He had expressed a wish that he could "live up to his blue china." His rooms in Magdalen, panelled and hung with engravings chosen for their difference from the pictures commonly affected, had been a centre of debate. His attitude had caused discussion and public protest, for he rode but did not hunt, did not play cricket, watched boat-races but did not go on the river, and only once showed much physical activity, when he wheeled Ruskin's barrow during the famous expedition of undergraduate navvies to make a road on Hinksey Marsh.[1]

[1] "The Æsthetic Movement in England," by Walter Hamilton.

We shall, perhaps, be better able to understand the first period of Wilde's public prominence, if we examine the origins of the movement of which, by accident and inclination, he became the accepted protagonist. Continental critics have noticed in his writings theories so closely analogous to those of the French Symbolists that they find it difficult not to believe that he was a disciple of that school, and, as it were, an English representative of Mallarmé's salon in the Rue de Rome. It is true that, like the Symbolists, he sought intensity in art, and emphasis of its potential at the expense of its kinetic qualities. But in this he was English as well as French. Later in his life he was influenced by Maeterlinck and by Huysmans, but, while he was at Oxford and for some time after, he found his rules of art and life in the teaching of the Pre-Raphaelites. That teaching represents a movement in the same direction as the Symbolists, but a movement which, unlike the French, came to be identified with a desire to bring ordinary life into harmony with the intensity it demanded from art.

It is worth while to gain a clear perspective by discovering the relation between such men as Morris, Burne-Jones, Rossetti, and Ruskin, and the cult of knee-breeches and chrysanthemums with which Punch and "Patience" identified Wilde. This cult was not a sudden sporadic flowering of strange blooms in the frail hands of a few undergraduates. It had its origin in 1849, when the members of the Pre-Raphaelite Brotherhood founded The Germ, an extraordinarily earnest little monthly magazine, in which appeared Rossetti's "Blessed Damozel," and etchings by Holman Hunt and Madox Brown. Perhaps, indeed, it had an earlier origin in the poetry of Keats, whose pure devotion to art for art's sake foreshadowed the feeling of the Pre-Raphaelite Brethren, or in the poetry of Blake, who, like them, emphasized the difference between the Sons of David and the Philistines. But, if we go back so far, we must go further and find still deeper roots for it in the great figures of the Romantic Movement, in the figures who made that movement possible, in Goethe, in Rousseau, in Ossian, in Percy's "Reliques of Ancient English Poetry." Wilde, at least, saw back thus far into his spiritual ancestry. But, in the middle of the nineteenth century, the

Pre-Raphaelites, refusing the abstract art whose beginnings are marked by the technical skill of Raphael, finding in early Italian painting, whose spirit was less hidden by clear and insistent letter, a vivifying principle, stood, not only for a new kind of painting, but for a new attitude towards art in general, and then for a new attitude towards life. They were attacked, and Ruskin, who thought they were trying to realize a prophecy of his own, came to aid them with eloquent defence. Their pictures were sold but seldom exhibited, so that a kind of separateness, almost a secrecy, came to belong to their admirers. The public in general looked upon them as something aloof and mad. It happened, perhaps through the accident of Miss Siddal and Mrs. William Morris so frequently sitting as their models, perhaps because these ladies exemplified what was already their ideal, that there came into many paintings what is best known as the Pre-Raphaelite woman, long-necked, and pomegranate-lipped. Nature, as Wilde was never tired of insisting, is assiduous in her imitation of art, and, when Sir Coutts Lindsay opened the Grosvenor Gallery for the benefit of these artists and their admirers, there were, beside those on the walls, a sufficient number of Pre-Raphaelite portraits walking about in the flesh to justify the curiosity and amusement of the crowd. A play, "The Colonel," of no great value, and the wholly delightful "Patience," a comic opera by Gilbert with music by Sullivan, brought the "greenery-yallery" gowns of the "Grosvenor Gallery" elect, with their poets and flowers and feelings towards the intenser life, into a charming masquerade. "Patience" was played at the Savoy with great success. Mr. D'Oyly Carte, attempting to repeat this success in America, perceived that Americans, being without a Grosvenor Gallery, missed much of the humour of the play, and conceived the Napoleonic scheme of sending over a specimen æsthete to show what "Patience" was laughing at. This somewhat ignominious position was, with due diplomacy, offered to Oscar Wilde, on account of his extravagance in dress,[1] and proudly accepted by him on the wilful supposition that it was a fitting tribute to his recently published *Poems*. That is how

[1] He wore at this time a velvet *béret* on his head, his shirts turned back with lace over his sleeves, puce velveteen knickerbockers with buckles, and black silk stockings.

it came about that on December 24, 1881, Wilde sailed for New York, to say that he was disappointed in the Atlantic, to tell the Customs Officials that he had nothing to declare except his genius, and to lecture throughout America on "The English Renaissance of Art," "House Decoration," and "Art and the Handicraftsman."

Youth and vanity helped to blind him to the rather humiliating reason of his lecturing. He wanted the money, but was able to persuade himself that he had really been chosen to represent the æsthetic movement to the American people on account of his book of poems, and that, in any case, he wanted to go to America to have *Vera*, a worthless melodrama he had just written, put upon the stage. With his happy power of dramatizing his position, a power he shared with Beau Brummel and picturesque adventurers of lesser genius, he saw himself, almost immediately, as a sort of combination of William Morris and John Ruskin, gifted more than they with wit, beauty, and youth. He spoke of himself visiting the South Kensington Museum on Saturday nights, "to see the handicraftsman, the wood-worker, the glassblower, and the worker in metals." He inspected art-schools, and carried away, to show his audiences, brass dishes beaten by little boys, and wooden bowls painted by little girls. He began to take himself more and more seriously—no doubt Punch's caricatures had helped him, and he was alone in America, far from the facts—and was able to tell his listeners "how it first came to me at all to create an artistic movement in England, a movement to show the rich what beautiful things they might enjoy and the poor what beautiful things they might create." By this time I have no doubt that he believed with perfect good faith that the æsthetic movement was the work and aim of his life. Only occasionally did he remember that he was living up to "Patience." "You have listened to 'Patience' for a hundred nights," he said, "and you have heard me for one only. It will make, no doubt, that satire more piquant by knowing something about the subject of it, but you must not judge of æstheticism by the satire of Mr. Gilbert." Once, indeed, he allowed himself to remind his audience of the extravagances at which that opera laughed, but then it was only to defend them with all the solemnity of an apostle. "You have heard, I think, a few of you, of two flowers connected with the æsthetic movement in England, and said (I assure you, erroneously) to be the food of some æsthetic young men. Well, let me tell you that the reason we love the lily and the sunflower, in spite of what Mr. Gilbert may tell you, is not for any vegetable fashion at all. It is because these two lovely flowers are in England the two most perfect models of design, the most naturally adapted for decorative art—the gaudy leonine beauty of the one and the precious loveliness of the other giving to the artist the most entire and perfect joy." This seems insufferable now, and probably was so then, but it is a proof of the perfection with which Wilde played the part his stage-manager had assigned him.

There is much that is charming in the lectures, together with much that is ridiculous, and some of the charm is in the folly. It is a very young knight who fights with a lily on his helmet and a sunflower tied to his spear-point. He has not perceived that the battle is at all difficult. He does not try with slow argument to undermine the enemy's position, but only says, quite cheerfully, that he would like to win. "When I was at Leadville and reflected that all the shining silver that I saw coming from the mines would be made into ugly dollars, it made me sad. It should be made into something more permanent. The golden gates at Florence are as beautiful to-day as when Michael Angelo saw them." He does not ever come to blows, but only says how ready he is for battle. "I have no respect," he quotes from Keats, "for the public, nor for anything in existence but the Eternal Being, the memory of great men and the principle of Beauty." And he shows that the great men are on his side. In one lecture alone he appeals to Goethe, Rousseau, Scott, Coleridge, Wordsworth, Blake, Homer, Dante, Morris, Keats, Chaucer, Hunt, Millais, Rossetti, Burne-Jones, Ruskin, Swinburne, Tennyson, Plato, Aristotle, Leonardo da Vinci, Edgar Allan Poe, Phidias, Michael Angelo, Sophocles, Milton, Fra Angelico, Rubens, Leopardi, Titian, Giorgione, Hugo, Balzac, Shakespeare, Mazzini, Petrarch, Baudelaire, Theocritus, and Gautier.

Indeed, his relation to the æsthetic movement of 1880 is not unlike that of Gautier to the Romantic movement of 1830. Gautier, like Wilde, was born into an army already on the march, and became its most violent champion and exemplar. Gautier's crimson waistcoat balances Wilde's knee-breeches. It would be possible to carry the comparison further, and to find in *Dorian Gray* a parallel to "Mademoiselle de Maupin." An identical spirit presided over the writing of both these books. And it would be easy to find in Wilde, at any rate before his release from prison, an aloofness from ordinary life not at all unlike that of the man who exclaimed, "Je suis un homme des temps homériques; —le monde où je vis n'est pas le mien, et je ne comprends rien à la société qui m'entoure." I can imagine Gautier lecturing Americans in just such a manner as Wilde's, and forgetting, but for his loyalty to Hugo, that he had not invented Romanticism.

Wilde's lectures must have amused if they did not edify America. He urged the miners to retain their high boots, their blouses, their sombreros, when, with wealth in their pockets, they should return to the abomination of civilization. Surprised audiences in the towns heard him speak seriously of the stolid ugliness of the horse-hair sofa, and still more seriously of stoves decorated with funeral urns in cast iron. He begged them to realize the importance of a definite scheme of colour in their rooms, and to use other kinds of jugs than one. In his independence of the quarrels of his elders, he talked to them as Ruskin might have talked, of the craftsman and his place in life, and, at the same time, praised the Peacock Room and the room in blue and yellow designed by that American whom Ruskin had accused of throwing a pot of paint in the public's face. On one or two occasions Americans were rude to him. But he spoke with such courtesy and such obvious benevolence that more often they were content to pay their dollars, listen to him attentively, stare at him curiously, and then go to see "Patience."

Wilde took their dollars, left the propagation of beautiful furniture behind him, and went to Paris. He was tired of prophecy and ready to take a new part in a new play. He had

". . . touched the tender stops of various quills,
With eager thought warbling his Doric lay."

and now, seeking the fresh woods of the Bois,

and the new pastures of the Champs Élysées, he "twitched his mantle" and threw it away, and with it sunflower, lily, and knee-breeches, preferring a change of costume with his change of part. He dressed now as a man of fashion, a dandy, but not an æsthete. He even cut his hair. But the reputation he had made swelled before him. He came to Paris, after his lecturing, in 1883, but, as late as 1891, for those who had not seen him, Wilde "n'était encore que celui qui fumait des cigarettes à bout d'or et qui se promenait dans les rues une fleur de tournesol à la main." He may even have encouraged this reputation. Stuart Merrill, writing in La Plume, said: "Certains cochers de hansom affirment même l'avoir vu se promener, vers l'heure des chats et des poètes, avec un lys enorme à la main. Oscar Wilde récuse comme à regret leur témoignage en répondant que la légende est souvent plus vraie que la réalité." But in 1883 Wilde had had a surfeit of lilies and sunflowers, and came to Paris as a poet, fashionably dressed, with a number of white vellum volumes of verse to distribute among those whose acquaintance he wished to secure.

He took rooms at the Hôtel Voltaire, and saw most of the better known people of the day. But, as always, he was not content to leave a part half played. He was in Paris as a poet, and, if he was ready to receive the poet's reward of admiration and homage, he was determined also to earn it, to write poetry, and not to rest on what he had already written. He was, at this time, impressed as much by Balzac's power of work as by his genius, and his biographer tells us that, with a view to imitating it, he wore, while working, a white robe with a hood, like the dressing-gown in which Balzac sat up at night, drinking coffee and creating his fiery world. He also walked out with an ivory stick, set with turquoises, like the stick that pleased Balzac because it set the town talking. At a later time he sought a similar adventitious aid to industry in buying Carlyle's writing-table. He felt, like Balzac, that the special paraphernalia of work was likely to induce the proper spirit. In these circumstances, in the Hôtel Voltaire, he finished *The Duchess of Padua*, and possibly either wrote or re-wrote *The Sphinx*.

*The Duchess of Padua* is a play on the

Elizabethan model of dark and bloody tragedy. It is a sombre spectacle, marred by a constantly shifting perspective. The folds of tragedy's cloak fall over an angular figure, a little stiff in the joints, and the verse has the effect of voluntary draping. It is the performance of a young man who has not yet achieved the knowledge of the stage that was later to be his; the performance of a young man who has not yet achieved a knowledge of himself. It is better built than *Vera* and more interesting, but it has the faults of the 1881 volume of *Poems*, without the same excuse of eager imitation and criticism. Here and there are lines of poetry that seem now afraid and now defiant of the progress of the play. The poet changes faces too often. He has all the Elizabethans at his back, and writes like the young Shakespeare on one page, and on the next like Shakespeare grown mature. His predilections are now for simplicity and now for such overworked **conceits** as this:—

"Guido.      Oh, how I love you!
See, I must steal the cuckoo's voice, and tell
This one tale over.

> Duchess.  Tell no other tale!
> For, if that is the little cuckoo's song,
> The nightingale is hoarse, and the loud lark
> Has lost its music."

Wilde's weakness of grip on himself and his play is shown by the quite purposeless inclusion of cumbersome, would-be-Shakespearean comic relief:—

> "Third Citizen. What think you of this young man who stuck the knife into the Duke?
>
> Second Citizen. Why, that he is a well-behaved, and a well-meaning, and a well-favoured lad, and yet wicked in that he killed the Duke.
>
> Third Citizen. 'Twas the first time he did it: maybe the law will not be hard on him, as he did not do it before."

This is a specimen very favourable to the play, which contains yet duller jokes. It is hard to believe that the same man who wrote them was also the author of *Intentions* and the inventor of Bunbury. But there is no need to linger over *The Duchess of Padua*, which, though it has moments of obscure power, Wilde did not, in later years, consider worthy of himself.

There is some doubt as to the date of composition of *The Sphinx.* A line and a half in it—

> "I have hardly seen
> Some twenty summers cast their green for Autumn's gaudy liveries"—

not only suggest extreme youth in the writer, but occur in *Ravenna.* Mr. Stuart Mason, in his admirable "Bibliography to the Poems of Oscar Wilde," says that "altogether some dozen passages of *Ravenna* are taken more or less verbatim from poems published before 1878, while no instance is found of lines in the Newdigate Prize Poem being repeated in poems admittedly of later date, and this," he thinks, "seems fairly strong proof that the lines in *The Sphinx* (if not the whole poem) antedate *Ravenna.*" Mr. Ross says that Wilde told him the poem was written at the Hôtel Voltaire during an earlier visit in 1874. This statement, he thinks, was an example of the poetic licence in which Wilde, like Shelley and other men of genius, was willing to indulge. Mr. Sherard says positively that Wilde wrote *The Sphinx* in 1883 at the Hôtel Voltaire. There seems to be no real reason why Wilde should not have borrowed from

*Ravenna* on this, even if he did so on no other occasion. He was always ready to seem younger than he was, and always ready to use again a phrase that had pleased him, no matter where he had used it before. In *The Duchess of Padua*, about whose date there is no question, he even went so far as to use two lines from a sonnet that he had previously addressed to Ellen Terry, and published in *Poems*:—

"O hair of gold, O crimson lips, O face
Made for the luring and the love of man!"

There is much in the poem itself that inclines me to trust Mr. Sherard's memory of its date.

It is work more personal to Wilde than anything in *Poems*. The firm mastery of its technique would, indeed, be overwhelming proof that it was written after *The Duchess of Padua* if it were not known that Wilde spent some time in revising it in 1889. But revision cannot alter the whole texture of a poem, and *The Sphinx* is full of those decorative effects that are rare in his very early work and give to much of his matured writing its most noticeable quality. No one has suggested that it was written later than 1883, so that we must explain the extraordinary advance that it shows on *The Duchess of Padua* as one of those curious phenomena known to most artists : it often happens that, in turning from one kind of work to another, as from dramatic writing to poetry, men come quite suddenly on what seem to be revised and better editions of themselves.

The kinetic base, the obvious framework, of *The Sphinx* is an apostrophe addressed by a student to a Sphinx that lies in his room, perhaps a dream, perhaps a paperweight, an apostrophe that consists in the enumeration of her possible lovers, and the final selection of one of them as her supposed choice. It is a series rather than a whole, though an effect of form and cumulative weight is given to it by a carefully preserved monotony. In a firm, lava-like verse, the Sphinx's paramours are stiffened to a bas-relief. The water-horse, the griffon, the hawk-faced god, the mighty limbs of Ammon, are formed into a frieze of reverie; they do not collaborate in a picture, but are left behind as the dream goes on. It goes on, perhaps, just a little too long. So do some of the finest rituals; and *The Sphinx* is among the rare incantations in our language. It is a piece of black magic. Of the student who saw such things men might well say:—

> "Weave a circle round him thrice,
> And close your eyes with holy dread,"

but they could never continue:—

> "For he on honey-dew hath fed,"

and, with whatever milk he had been nourished, they would be certain that it was not that of Paradise.

> "Dawn follows Dawn and Nights grow old, and all
>     the while this curious cat
> Lies crouching on the Chinese mat with eyes of
>     satin rimmed with gold."

To paint the visions she inspires, Wilde ransacks the world for magnificent colouring. He does not always secure magnificence in the noblest way, but is satisfied with an opulence, rather of things than of emotion, brought bodily into the verse and not suggested by the proud stepping of the mind. Cleopatra's wine, ivory-bodied Antinous, the crocodile with jewelled ears, metal-flanked gryphons, gilt-scaled dragons,

# ÆSTHETICISM

"Some Nereid coiled in amber foam with curious rock-
   crystal breasts,"

the Ethiopian, "whose body was of polished
jet," Pasht "who had green beryls for her
eyes," Horus,

"Whose wings, like strange transparent talc, rose high
   above his hawk-faced head,
Painted with silver and with red and ribbed with rods
   of Oreichalch,"

the marble limbs of Ammon, "on pearl and
porphyry pedestalled," an ocean emerald on
his ivory breast—

"The merchants brought him steatite from Sidon in their
   painted ships:
The meanest cup that touched his lips was fashioned
   from a chrysolite——"

the lion's "long flanks of polished brass," the
tiger's "amber sides":—I think it is worth
while to notice the mineral character of all
this imagery. It is as if a man were finding
solace for his feverish hands in the touch
of cool hard stones, and at the same time,
stimulating his fever by the sexual excitement of contrast between the over-sensitive
and the utterly insensible.

F

Wilde had but a short respite from the trouble of keeping up a reputation and an income. The American dollars were soon spent, and he had to bring to an end his Balzacian industry, and the delightful business of being a poet in Paris. He returned to London, where he took rooms in Charles Street, Haymarket. He had to earn a livelihood, and poverty and his own extravagance compelled him to do that which he most disliked, to take up again a pose whose fascination he had exhausted. He signed an agreement with a lecture agency, and toured through the English provinces, repeating, as cheerfully as he could, the lectures he had given in America.

## NOTE ON WILDE AND WHISTLER

Both before and after his American lecturing tour Wilde was one of the frequenters of Whistler's studio in Chelsea. He had an unbounded admiration for this painter, whose conversation was no less vivid than his work, and Whistler's attitude towards him was not so cavalier as that he adopted to others among his admirers. Wilde, in spite of his youth, had a reputation, and shared with Whistler the applause of any company in which they were together. In 1883, when Wilde was to lecture to the Academy Students, he asked Whistler what he should say to them. Whistler sketched a lecture for him, and Wilde used parts of it with success and repaid him by a tremendous compliment. Two years later Whistler himself lectured, and, for his "Ten O'Clock," re-appropriated some of the material he had suggested to his friend. That is the origin of the accusation, so often made, that Wilde built a reputation on borrowed bons mots. In the "Ten O'Clock," Whistler, annoyed by Wilde's lecturing on art, as he would have been by the lecturing of any other man who was not himself a painter, held a veiled figure of him up to ridicule, and threw a stone from a frail house in jeering at his knee-breeches. "Costume is not dress. And the wearers of wardrobes may not be doctors of taste . . ." Wilde smilingly replied. Whistler feinted. Wilde parried. Whistler thrust :—" What has Oscar in common with Art except that he dines at our tables and picks from our platters the plums for the pudding that he peddles in the provinces? Oscar—the amiable, irresponsible, esurient Oscar—with no more sense of a picture than he has of the fit of a coat—has the courage of the opinions . . . of others!" Wilde answered that "with our James vulgarity begins at home and should be allowed to stay there," and with that their friendship was buried, like the hatchet, "in the side of the enemy." Two years later, Wilde, with an indifference amusing in any case and delightful if it was conscious, roused further protest by using in 'The Decay of Lying' the phrase, "the courage of the opinions of others," that had been the sting of Whistler's reproach. The letters on both sides may be read in "The Gentle Art of Making Enemies." The whole story only makes it clear that

Wilde was better able to appreciate Whistler than Whistler to appreciate a younger man, whose talent, no less brilliant, was entirely different from his own. As Mr. Ross has pointed out, all Wilde's best work was written after their friendship ceased.

# V

## MISCELLANEOUS PROSE

ON May 29, 1884, Oscar Wilde was married to Constance Mary Lloyd, the daughter of an eminent barrister. He settled with her in Chelsea. They had two children, both boys, born respectively in 1885 and 1886.

He supplemented his wife's income by writing reviews of books for the Pall Mall Gazette, and articles on the theatre for The Dramatic Review. From the autumn of 1887 to that of 1889 he edited The Woman's World. Little of this was wasted labour, though Wilde had no need to fillip his invention by such practice as the writing of reviews provided. Conversation was to him what diaries, note-books, and hack-work are to so many others. But there is an ease in the essays of *Intentions* wholly lacking in 'The Rise of Historical Criticism' and in the lectures. It is impossible not to believe that in writing literary notes in The Woman's World and reviews in The Pall Mall Gazette, he quickened the turn of his wrist and sharpened the point of his rapier.

There is little of any great value in the volume of reviews collected by his executor; little, that is to say, that raises them above the level of reviews written by far less gifted men. Here and there are fragments that he improved and used again in more lasting works. Here and there are perfectly charming sentences, that show what sort of man would be found if we could lift the mask of the reviewer. Throughout the book are uncertain indications of the theories of art that were later to be expounded in *Intentions*. But that is all. There is, however, an historical interest in learning what Wilde thought of the writers of his time. He railed at the shocking bad grammar of Professor Saintsbury, and got an undergraduate enjoyment from laughing at Professor Mahaffy. When he could, he piously drew attention to the works of his father and mother. He was polite to his cousin, W. G. Wills, who happened to be delivered of an epic. Among greater men, he had excellent praise for William Morris, a just appreciation of Pater, an enthusiasm for Meredith, the expression of which he afterwards used in *Intentions*, and a perspicuous criticism of Swinburne. The volume is full of clues to the sources of the inessentials in his later work. The original of the passage in *Dorian Gray* on embroideries and tapestries is to be found in a review of a book by Ernest Lefébure. The Star-child's curls " were like the rings of the daffodil." This curious and delightful phrase may be traced to a review of Morris' translation of the Odyssey, where Wilde noticed the line,

> "With the hair on his head crisp curling as the bloom of the daffodil,"

and quoted another version published in 1665,

> "Minerva renders him more tall and fair,
> Curling in rings like daffodils his hair."

It would be possible to make a long list of such alibis.

Marriage and journalism slackened for a moment his ambition. He lectured once or twice, though Whistler had almost succeeded in discrediting him as an authority upon art. His reputation waned, and he was for some time a young man with a brilliant past. Art seemed less worth while than it had been, and he was ready to amuse himself with things that he thought scarcely worth writing, things that required more cleverness than temperament, and did not stretch his genius. It was in this mood that he turned to narrative, and wrote the four stories which, published in magazines in 1887, were collected into a volume in 1891. He had always been accustomed to invent plots for other people, and to compose such anecdotes as were needed to illustrate his conversation and to give it an historical basis. Mr. Sherard says that he used to devise stories, sometimes as many as six in a morning, for his brother William to write. It occurred to him to write some of these tales himself, and, using the conventions of the popular magazine fiction of his day, yet find means to indulge his mind with the ingenious play in which it delighted. Three of these tales need detain no student of Wilde. 'The Canterville Ghost' is just so boisterous as to miss its balance, but, because it is about Americans, is very popular in America. 'The Sphinx without a Secret' betrays its secret in its title. 'The Model

Millionaire' is an empty little thing no better than the popular tales it tries to imitate. 'Lord Arthur Savile's Crime,' however, is not only remarkable as an indication of what Wilde was to do both as a dramatist and as a storyteller, but is itself a delightful piece of buffoonery. Wilde is so serious. The readers of The Family Herald are fond of lords, and so the story begins with a reception at Bentinck House, a delightful parody of the popular descriptions of such a function. "It was certainly a wonderful medley of people. Gorgeous peeresses chatted affably to violent Radicals, popular preachers brushed coat-tails with eminent sceptics, a perfect bevy of bishops kept following a stout prima-donna from room to room, on the staircase stood several Academicians, disguised as artists, and it was said at one time the supper-room was absolutely crammed with geniuses." There was a cheiromantist, and a Duchess, who, on learning that he was present, " began looking about for a small tortoiseshell fan and a very tattered lace shawl, so as to be ready to go at a moment's notice." The plot is no less moral than simple. Lord Arthur Savile learns from the palmist that at some period of his life it is decreed that he shall commit a murder. Unwilling to marry while a potential criminal, he sets about committing the murder at once, to get it over, and be able to marry with the easy conscience of one who knows that his duty has been satisfactorily performed. He tries to kill a charming aunt with a sugared pill, and a benevolent uncle with an explosive clock, and, failing in both these essays, " oppressed with the barrenness of good intentions," walks miserably on the Embankment, where he finds Mr. Podgers, the cheiromantist, observing the river. "A brilliant idea flashed across him, and he stole softly up behind. In a moment he had seized Mr. Podgers by the legs, and flung him into the Thames. There was a coarse oath, a heavy splash, and all was still. Lord Arthur looked anxiously over, but could see nothing of the cheiromantist but a tall hat, pirouetting in an eddy of moonlit water. After a time it also sank, and no trace of Mr. Podgers was visible. Once he thought that he caught sight of the bulky misshapen figure striking out for the staircase by the bridge, and a horrible feeling of failure came over him, but it turned out to be merely a reflection, and when the moon shone out from behind a cloud it passed away. At last he seemed to have realised the decree of destiny. He heaved a deep sigh of relief, and Sybil's name came to his lips." Like much of Wilde's work, this story is very clever talk, an elaborated anecdote, told with flickering irony, a cigarette now and again lifted to the lips. But, already, a dramatist is learning to use this irony in dialogue, and a decorative artist is restraining his buoyant cleverness, to use it for more subtle purposes. There is a delicate description of dawn in Piccadilly, with the waggons on their way to Covent Garden, white-smocked carters, and a boy with primroses in a battered hat, riding a big grey horse—a promise of the fairy stories. The vegetables against the sky are masses of jade, "masses of green jade against the pink petals of some marvellous rose." And, too, over the sudden death of Mr. Podgers "the moon peered through a mane of tawny clouds, as if it were a lion's eye, and innumerable stars spangled the hollow vault, like gold dust powdered on a purple dome."

*The Happy Prince and other Tales*, published in 1888, with pictures by Jacomb Hood and Walter Crane, are very married stories. In reading them, I cannot help feeling that Wilde wrote one of them as an experiment, to show, I suppose, that he could have been Hans Andersen if he had liked, and his wife importuned him to make a book of things so charming, so good, and so true. He made the book, and there is one beautiful thing in it, 'The Happy Prince,' which was, I suspect, the first he wrote. The rest, except, perhaps, 'The Selfish Giant,' a delightful essay in Christian legend, are tales whose morals are a little too obvious even for grown-up people. Children are less willing to be made good. Wilde was himself perfectly aware of his danger, and, no doubt, got some pleasure out of saying so, at the end of the story called 'The Devoted Friend': "'I am rather afraid that I have annoyed him,' answered the Linnet. 'The fact is, that I told him a story with a moral.' 'Ah! that is always a very dangerous thing to do,' said the Duck. And I quite agree with her." There is a moral in 'The Happy Prince,' but there is this difference between that story and the others, that it is quite clear that Wilde wanted to write it. It is Andersen, treated exactly as Wilde treated Milton in the volume of 1881, only with more assurance, and a greater certainty about his own contribution. We recognize Wilde by the decorative effects that are scattered throughout the book. He preferred a lyrical pattern to a prosaic perspective, and, even more than his wit, his love of decoration is the distinguishing quality of his work. Andersen might well have invented the story of the swallow who died to repay the statue for jewelled eyes and gold-leaf mail given to the poor of the town of which he had once been the Happy and unseeing Prince, but he would never have let the swallow say: "The King is there in his painted coffin. He is wrapped in yellow linen and embalmed in spices. Round his neck is a chain of pale green jade, and his hands are withered leaves." And only a swallow belonging to the author of *The Sphinx* would have said, "To-morrow my friends will fly up to the second Cataract. The river horse couches there among the bulrushes, and on a great granite throne sits the God Memnon. All night long he watches the stars, and when the morning star shines he utters one cry of joy, and then he is silent. At noon the yellow lions come down to the water's edge to drink. They have eyes like green beryls, and their roar is louder than the roar of the Cataract."

In the next year he was again amusing himself with fairy tales, writing this time a book alone in English literature; a book of tales not intended for the British child but for those grown-up people who shared Wilde's own enjoyment of brilliant-coloured fantasy. He had learnt to control his invention, although he did not choose to do without a tuning-fork. Andersen still struck the note to which Wilde sang, but Flaubert had been his singing master, and the curious and beautiful tales collected in *A House of Pomegranates* are like what I imagine "The Snow Queen" would have been, if it had been written by the author of "Saint Julien l'Hospitalier." In 'The Infanta's Birthday,' where one of Goya's grotesques dances before a painting by Velasquez, the flowers pass their opinions on the dwarf quite in the Danish manner. In 'The Star-child': " 'The Earth is going to be married, and this is her bridal dress,' whispered the Turtle-doves to each other. Their little pink feet were quite frost-bitten, but they felt that it was their duty to

take a romantic view of the situation." That
is surely written by the ghost of Andersen's
English translator. But 'The Star-child'
ends with the firm, aloof touch of Flaubert,
who would not tolerate "quite": "Yet ruled
he not long, so great had been his suffering,
and so bitter the fire of his testing, for after
the space of three years, he died. And he
who came after him ruled evilly." I remember
the end of "Hérodias" on just such a distant
note: "Et tous les trois, ayant pris la tête de
Iaokanaan, s'en allèrent du côté de la Galilée.
Comme elle était très lourde, ils la portaient
alternativement." And the picture of the
leper in this story is almost a transcription of
that in "Saint Julien l'Hospitalier": "Over
his face hung a cowl of grey linen, and
through the eyelits his eyes gleamed like red
coals." And Flaubert: "Il était enveloppé
d'une toile en lambeaux, la figure pareille à
un masque de platre et les deux yeux plus
rouge que des charbons." I do not suggest
that one is a copy of the other; but I think
that Wilde remembered that clay mask with
gleaming eyes, and mistook it for a creation
of his own whose eyes shone through a grey
linen cowl.

It is hardly worth while so to carry the study of influence into detail. Wilde wrote, with the pen of Flaubert, stories that might have been imagined by Andersen, and sometimes one and sometimes the other touches his hand. It is not impossible that Baudelaire was also present. But all this does not much concern us, except that by subtraction we may come to what we seek, which is the personal, elusive, but unmistakable quality contributed by Wilde himself.

This is, secondarily, a round mellowness of voice, a smooth solidity of suggested movement, a delight in magnificence; and, primarily, a wonderful feeling for decorative effect. This last is Wilde's peculiar contribution to literature. His contribution to thought, his exegesis of the critical attitude, is another matter. But this feeling for decoration, that made him see life itself as a tapestry of ordered and beautiful movements caught in gold and dyed silk, that made him incapable of realizing that life was not so, until at last it became too strong and tore his canvas, was itself enough to prevent the picturesque figure of the dandy from obliterating the artist in the minds of posterity. It is scarcely twenty years since Wilde wrote his books, and, in poetry as well as in prose, their influence is already becoming so common as not to be recognized. The historian of the period will have to trace what he may call "The Decorative Movement in Literature" to the works of Wilde, and through them to the Pre-Raphaelite pictures and poems, whose ideals he so fantastically misrepresents.

I have implied a distinction between decoration and realism that I have not clearly defined. This distinction is not, though it has often been held to be, a distinction between two different kinds of art, between which runs a sharp dividing line. It is rather a recognition of opposite ends of a scale, like the recognition of heat and cold, both degrees of temperature, but without intrinsic superiority one over the other. In painting we thus distinguish between the attempt to imitate and the willingness (not the intention) to suggest nature. This distinction is best expressed in the old simile of the window and the wall. Some pictures represent a pattern on a wall: some pictures represent a vision through a window. In some we look at the canvas: in others we look through the frame. Some are decorative: some are realistic. Many painters have wished that their pictures should not be found wanting when compared with the pictures of similar subjects that each spectator paints with the brushes and palette of his own brain. Sometimes this desire has been carried so far as to preclude all others. Painters do not usually read Berkeley, and there have been some who forgot that there was no such thing as a world outside their brains, and cared only to be recognized as faithful portrait-painters of nature: that is to say, of what all spectators see, or can see, by training their observation. There have been critics, too, like Ruskin, who have chosen to compare painters by their fidelity to this external and observable nature. But painters have other things to do than photograph, other things to do than to select from what a camera would represent. Sometimes the idea of imitation fades away, and they are willing, no more, to suggest lilies by a convention, and to distort even the human figure, while they concern themselves with harmonies in which the shapes of flower or figure sound merely incidental notes. We must not forget that these are extremes in a single scale, and that all painting is to some extent realistic, to some extent decorative. Its extremes are wholly imitative in aim, and dull, and wholly conventional in aim, and empty. We call the two aims realism and decoration for our convenience. In literature it is possible to trace a similar double aim, separate from but analogous to the duality in speech that we shall have to examine in a later chapter. There are books subservient to what we call reality, and books for which reality is no more than an excuse, books that follow nature, and books that cast nature into their own mould, and, delighting in no accidental harmonies, bend nature to the patterns that please them, and heighten or lower her colours for their private purposes of beautiful creation. Even in music we can trace these tendencies: there is music that humbly follows the moods of man, and music whose serenely indifferent patterns compel the dancing attendance of those moods.

We have observed in *The Sphinx* the decorative character of Wilde's work. These tales provide the best examples of it that are to be found in his prose. To the woodcutters looking down from the forest, the Earth seemed "like a flower of silver, and the Moon like a flower of gold." The young fisherman speaks to the witch of his "*painted* boat," and his author is no less aloof from realism. When the young fisherman forgets his nets and his cunning, as he listens to the sweet voice of the mermaid, Wilde writes: "Vermilion finned and with eyes of bossy gold, the tunnies went by in shoals, but he heeded them not." Now that is a picture that the young fisherman could not see. Nor can we see it, unless the fisherman is a figure on a tapestry, sewn in stitches of bright-coloured thread. Above him three undulating lines are waves, and between them four tunnies, twisting unanimous tails, show their vermilion fins and their eyes of gilded metal, skilfully bedded in the canvas.

Wilde, always perfectly self-conscious, was not unaware of this difference between his own writing and that of most of his contemporaries. When *Dorian Gray* was attacked for immorality, Wilde wrote, in a letter to a paper: "My story is an essay on decorative art. It reacts against the brutality of plain realism." *The Picture of Dorian Gray* was written for publication in a magazine. Six chapters were added to it to make it long enough for publication as a novel, because those who buy books, like those who buy pictures, are unable to distinguish between size and quality, and imagine that value depends upon area. The preface was written to answer assailants of the morality of the story in its first form, and included only when it was printed as a book. These circumstances partly explain the lack of proportion, and of cohesion, that mars, though it does not spoil, the first French novel to be written in the English language. England has a traditional novel-form with which even the greatest students of human comedy and tragedy square their work. In France there is no such tradition, with the result that the novel is a plastic form, moulded in the most various ways by the most various minds. After all, it is a question of name, and it is impossible without elaborate and tedious qualification to discuss classifications of literature. They should not be made, or they should be made differently, for, at present, they deal only with superficial resemblances, depending, sometimes, upon nothing more essential than the price for which a book is sold. They have, however, a distinct influence upon production. In France, Flaubert's "Tentation de Saint Antoine," that wonderful dream in which so many strange dialogues are overheard, Remy de Gourmont's "Une Nuit au Luxembourg," that delightful speculative mirage, and Huysmans' "À Rebours," that phantasmagoria of intellectual experience, are all included in publishers' lists of novels and sold as such. Publishers in England are not so catholic. Whatever the reason may be, economical, depending upon the publisher, traditional, depending on the writer, Wilde's *The Picture of Dorian Gray* was the first novel for many years to be written in England with that freedom in choice of matter and manner that has for a long time been in no way extraordinary in France. It has, so far, had no successor free as itself from the enforced interest in a love affair, to which we have grown so mournfully accustomed.

The story of the book is a fantastic invention like that of Balzac's "Le Peau de Chagrin," in which the scrap of skin from a wild ass shrinks with each wish of its possessor. The picture of Dorian Gray, painted by his friend, ages with the lines of cruelty, lust and hypocrisy that should mar its ever-youthful subject. He, remaining as beautiful as when at twenty-one he had inspired the painter with a masterpiece, walks in the ways of men, sullying his soul, whose bodily reflection records neither his age nor his sins. It is the sort of invention that would have pleased Hawthorne, and the book itself is written with the marked ethical sympathy that Wilde, in his preface, denounced as "an unpardonable mannerism of style." Perhaps the reason why it was so loudly accused of immorality was that in the popular mind luxury and sin are closely allied, and the unpardonable mannerism that made him preach, in a parable, against the one, did not hide his whole-hearted delight in describing the other.

The preface, inspired by the hostility the book aroused, is an essay not in the gentle art of making enemies, but in that of annoying them when made. If his critics tell him that his book leers with the eyes of foulness and dribbles with the lips of prurience, Wilde replies, with an ambiguity as disturbing as his smile, that "it is the spectator, and not life, that art really mirrors," and again that "the highest, as the lowest form of criticism is a mode of autobiography." His arrows are not angrily tipped with poison, but are not for that the less displeasing to those against whom they are directed. They are weighted not with anger but with æsthetic theory. They are so far separate from the story that they are best discussed with the essays of *Intentions*.

There are a few strange books that share the magic of some names, like Cornelius Agrippa, Raymond Lully, and Paracelsus, names that possibly mean more to us before than after we have investigated the works and personalities that lie behind them. These books are mysterious and kept, like mysteries, for peculiar moods. They are not books for every day, nor even for every night. We keep them for rare moments, as we keep in a lacquer cabinet some crystal-shrined thread of subtle perfume, or some curious gem, to be a solace in a mood that does not often recur, or, perhaps, to be an instrument in its evocation. *Dorian Gray*, for all its faults, is such a book. It is unbalanced;

and that is a fault. It is a mosaic hurriedly made by a man who reached out in all directions and took and used in his work whatever scrap of jasper, or porphyry or broken flint was put into his hand; and that is not a virtue. But in it there is an individual essence, a private perfume, a colour whose secret has been lost. There are moods whose consciousness that essence, perfume, colour, is needed to intensify.

There is little need to discuss the minutiæ of the book; to point out that its sayings occur in Wilde's plays, poems, reviews and dialogues; that it is, as it were, an epitome of his wit before and after the fact; that the eleventh chapter is a wonderful condensation of a main theme in " À Rebours," like an impression of a concerto rendered by a virtuoso upon a violin. There is no need to emphasize Wilde's delight in colour and fastidious luxury, as well as in a most amusing kind of dandyism: in the opening scene the studio curtains are of tussore silk, the dust is golden that dances in the sunlight, tea is poured from a fluted Georgian urn, there is a heavy scent of roses, the blossoms of the laburnum are honey-coloured as well as honey-sweet, Lord

Henry Wotton reclines on a divan of Persian saddlebags, and taps "the toe of his patent-leather boot with a tasselled ebony cane." There is no need to point out any of these things, but they help to justify what I have already said, and to define the indefinable character of the book. Lord Henry Wotton would have liked to write "a novel that would be as lovely as a Persian carpet, and as unreal." Wilde tried to write it, and very nearly succeeded.

. . . . . .

Wilde's second period of swift development began towards the end of 1888. This, perhaps, explains the sentence in 'Pen, Pencil, and Poison'—"One can fancy an intense personality being created out of sin." His personality was, certainly, intensified when he became an habitual devotee of the vice for which he was imprisoned. He had first experimented in that vice in 1886; his experiments became a habit in 1889, and in that year he published 'Pen, Pencil, and Poison,' and 'The Decay of Lying,' revised *The Sphinx*, and wrote some, at least, of the stories in *A House of Pomegranates*; these were immediately followed by 'The Critic as Artist,' and *Salomé*.

These things are among his best work. It is possible that a consciousness of separation from the common life of men is a sufficient explanation of an increased vividness in a man's self, a heightened ardour of production. Is Wilde's exceptional activity in those years to be attributed to an eagerness to justify himself by other men's admiration, of which he had never been careless? Was he eager to bring mankind to his side? "It is the spectator, not life, that art really mirrors." This sentence must now be applied to himself, when we consider 'The Portrait of Mr. W. H.' That narrative, now printed at the end of *Lord Arthur Savile's Crime*, and first published in Blackwood's Magazine in 1889, is an essay in criticism.

Wilde read something of himself into Shakespeare's sonnets, and, in reading, became fascinated by a theory that he was unable to prove. Where another man would, perhaps, have written a short, serious essay, and whistled his theory down the wind that carries the dead leaves of Shakespeare's commentators, Wilde tosses it as a belief between three brains, and allows it to unfold itself as the background to a story. The three brains are the narrator, Cyril Graham, and Erskine. Graham discovers the Mr. W. H. of the sonnets in a boy-actor called Will Hughes, and by diligent examination of internal evidence, almost persuades Erskine to believe him. Erskine, however, demands a proof, and Graham finds one for him in a portrait of Will Hughes nailed to an old wooden chest. Erskine is persuaded, but discovers that the picture is a forgery, whereupon Graham, explaining that he had only had it made for Erskine's satisfaction, leaves the picture to his friend, protests that the forgery in no way invalidates the theory, and kills himself as a proof of his good faith. Erskine, disbelieving, tells all this to the narrator, who instantly sets to work on the sonnets, finds a quantity of further evidence, but none that sets beyond question the existence in Elizabethan times of a boy-actor called William Hughes. He writes Erskine a letter of passionate reasoning, that, while persuading Erskine, wipes away his own belief. He finds that he has become an infidel to the theory of which he has been a successful advocate. It was a favourite idea of Wilde's, and the motive of *La Sainte Courtisane*, that to slough off a belief like a snake's skin, one has only to convert someone else to it. I need not further analyse the story, which is merely the mechanism that Wilde used for the display of the evidence to which he desired to draw attention.

It would be impossible to build an airier castle in Spain than this of the imaginary William Hughes; impossible, too, to build one so delightfully designed. The prose and the reasoning seem things of ivory, Indian-carved, through which the rarest wind of criticism may freely blow and carry delicate scents away without disturbing the yet more delicate fabric. Wilde assumes that Shakespeare addressed the sonnets to William Hughes, and, that assumption granted (though there is no William Hughes to be found), colours his theory with an abundance of persuasive touches, to strengthen what is, at first, only a courtesy belief. Though all his argument is special pleading, Wilde contrives to make you feel that counsel knows, though he cannot prove, that his client is in the right. The evidence is only for the jury. You are inclined to interrupt him with the exclamation that you are already convinced. But it is a pleasure to listen to him, so you let him go on. After all, " brute reason is quite unbearable. There is something unfair about its use. It is like hitting below the intellect." Wilde's 'Portrait of Mr. W. H.' is more than a refutable theory, a charming piece of speculation. It is an illustration of the critic as artist, a foretaste of *Intentions*. It is better than 'The Truth of Masks,' as good as 'The Decay of Lying.' Yet it was not printed in that book, where it might well have had a place. The reason for this is not uninteresting. Wilde did not intend to reprint it as it stood. The theory beneath that delicate brain-play had a lasting fascination for him, and, with its proofs, grew in its mind till it overbalanced Cyril Graham and doubting Erskine. He re-wrote it at greater length, after delays. When he was arrested, the publishers, who had already announced it as a forthcoming book, returned it to his house, whence it disappeared on the day of the enforced sale of his effects. It has never been recovered.

# VI

## INTENTIONS

MRS. MALAPROP classes paradoxes with Greek, Hebrew, simony and fluxions as inflammatory branches of learning, and, in *De Profundis*, Wilde says: "What the paradox was to me in the sphere of thought, perversity became to me in the realm of passion." Paradox and perversity were matches to set fire to his thought and his dreams. But paradox is not in itself different from direct speech. It is made by the statement of a result and the omission of the steps of reasoning by which that result has been achieved. When somebody accused Jean Moréas, that brilliant Greek, of being paradoxical, he replied: "I do not know what paradox is; I believe it is the name which imbeciles give to the truth." Wilde might have made a similar answer, and perhaps did. His paradoxes are only unfamiliar truths. Those of them that were thought the wildest are already becoming obvious, for unfamiliarity is a temporal quality like flowers in a road: when a multitude has passed that way the flowers are trodden out of sight. Paradox is, however, a proof of vitality and adventurous thought, and these things are sometimes the companions of charm. Unfamiliar truth was, at first, the most noticeable characteristic of Wilde's *Intentions*, but, though paradox may fade to commonplace, "age cannot wither nor custom stale" the fresh and debonair personality that keeps the book alive, tossing thoughts like roses, and playing with them in happiness of heart.

There is something of the undergraduate about the book. Its pages might be reprinted from a college magazine in which a genius was stretching youthful limbs, instead of from such staid and respectable reviews as The Fortnightly and The Nineteenth Century. It belongs to the days when the most natural thing in life is to talk until "the dusky night rides down the sky," and the pale morning light mocks at our yellow lamp. Indeed, I think that such freshness and vivacity of writing is the gift of those authors who are also talkers. They are accustomed to see their sentences in company, not in solitude. They give them a pleasing strut and swagger and teach them to make graceful entries and exits neither too ceremonious nor yet disorderly. Their sentences are men of the world, and of a world where the passport to success is charm. It is not so with lecturers or preachers, whose office puts them in a different category. But men who talk for their own enjoyment and for that of those who listen to them are less likely than others to compose by eye instead of by ear. It is actually difficult to read Wilde in silence. His sentences lift the voice as well as the thoughts of the writer from the printed page.

Wilde loved speech for its own sake, and nothing could be more characteristic of his gift than his choice of that old and inexhaustible form that Plato, Lucian, Erasmus and Landor, to name only a few, have turned to such different purposes. Dialogue is at once personal and impersonal. "By its means he (the thinker) can both reveal and conceal himself, and give form to every fancy, and reality to every mood. By its means he can exhibit the object from each point of view, and show it us in the round, as a sculptor shows us things, gaining in this manner all the richness and reality of effect that comes from those side issues that are suddenly suggested by the central idea in its progress, and really illumine the idea more completely, or from those felicitous afterthoughts that give a fuller completeness to the central scheme, and yet convey something of the delicate charm of chance." Nothing could better describe Wilde's own essays in dialogue.

The first of these essays is 'The Decay of Lying,' in which a young gentleman called Vivian reads aloud an article on that subject to a slightly older and rather incredulous young gentleman called Cyril, commenting as he reads, answering objections, and sometimes laying the manuscript on his knees as he follows the swift-flying swallow of his thought through the airy mazes of her joyous exercise. Vivian holds a brief for the artist against the nature that he is supposed to imitate. He behaves like a lawyer, first picking his opponent to pieces, lest the jury should be prejudiced in his favour, and then proving his own case in so far as it is possible to prove it. The dialogue is a delightful thing in itself: it is also of the first importance to the student of Wilde's theories of art. Under its insouciance and extravagance lie many of the ideas that dictated his attitude as writer and as critic. Vivian begins by opposing the comfort of a Morris chair to the discomfort of nature's insect-ridden grass, and complains that nature is as indifferent to her cultured critic as to cow or burdock—which is not to be borne. He then, a little more seriously, envisages the history of art as a long warfare between the simian instinct of imitation and the god-like instinct of self-expression. He needs to show that fine art does not imitate, and points out that Japanese painting, of which, at that time, everybody was talking, does not concern itself with Japan, and that the Japan we imagine for ourselves with the help of willow-pattern plates and the drawings of Hokusai is no more real in one sense and no less real in another than the slit-eyed girl of Gautier's "Chinoiserie," who lives in a porcelain tower above the Yellow River and the long-necked cormorants. Our ideal Japan has existed only in the minds of the artists who saw it, and when we cross the seas to look for it, we find nothing but a few fans and coloured lanterns. But that is not enough. We continually see lovely things in nature, strangely like the things we see in books and pictures. There is plagiary here, on one side or on the other, and, with almost ecstatic courage, Vivian announces that, so far from art holding the mirror to nature (a view advanced by Hamlet as a proof of his insanity), nature imitates art. He may have taken the hint from Musset, for Fortunio, in the comedy of that name, exclaims with melancholy criticism: " Comme ce soleil couchant est manqué ce soir. Regarde moi un peu ce vallée là-bas, ces quatre ou cinq méchants nuages qui grimpent sur cette montagne. Je faisais des paysages comme celui-là, quand j'avais douze ans, sur la couverture de mes livres de classe." But he made the statement in no spirit of extravagance. It seemed to him that we observed in nature what art has taught us to see, and he chose that way of saying so. He elaborates it delightfully, so that people may forget he has spoken the truth. Fogs, for example, did not exist till art had invented them. "Now, it must be admitted, fogs are carried to excess. They have become the mere mannerism of a clique, and the exaggerated realism of their method gives dull people bronchitis." Then he runs on for a few pages, illustrating these wise saws with modern and ingenious instances of life hurrying after fiction, reproducing the opening of "Dr. Jekyll and Mr. Hyde," setting an unreal Becky Sharp beside Thackeray's creation, and going so far, indeed, as to trip up the heels of a serial story with the sordid actuality of fact.

He discusses Zola and his no less heavy-footed disciples, who stand for the failure of imitation and are the best proofs that the mirror cracks when the artist holds it up to anything except himself. Cyril suggests that Balzac was a realist, and Vivian quotes Baudelaire's saying, that "his very scullions have genius," compares him to Holbein, and points out that he is far more real than life. "A steady course of Balzac reduces our living friends to shadows and our acquaintances to the shadows of shades."

Then comes an objection to modernity of form, and some reasons for that objection that suggest a very interesting speculation. He thinks that Balzac's love for modernity of form prevented him from producing any single book that can rank with the masterpieces of romantic art. And then:—"The public imagine that, because they are interested in their immediate surroundings, Art should be interested in them also, and should take them as her subject matter. But the mere fact that they are interested in these things makes them an unsuitable subject for Art. The only beautiful things, as somebody once said, are the things that do not concern us. As long as a thing is useful or necessary to us, or affects us in any way, either for pain or for pleasure, or appeals strongly to our sympathies, or is a vital part of the environment in which we live, it is outside the proper sphere of Art." These words seemed, in 1889, to be both daring and precarious. The influence of philosophy is not so immediate as is sometimes supposed. It is not extravagant to find in those few words a reflection, direct or indirect, of Immanuel Kant, who, writing in 1790, said that what is called beautiful is the object of a delight apart from any interest, and showed that charm, or intimate reference to our own circumstances or possible circumstances, so far from being a criterion of beauty, was a disturbing influence upon our judgment. In the Preface to *Dorian Gray*, that little flaunting compendium of Wilde's æsthetics, it is easy to trace the ideas of Kant, divested of their technical phrasing, freed from their background of reasoning and their foreground of accurate explanation. For example:—"No artist desires to prove anything." This balances Kant's banishment of concepts from the beautiful. For another:—" All art is quite useless." This balances Kant's distinction between the beautiful and the good. This is not the place for any worthy discussion of the relation between the theory and the practice of art; but it is interesting to notice that what was temperamentally true for Wilde, and therefore peculiarly his own, had been logically true for a philosopher a hundred years before. Coleridge, whose originality there is no more need to question than Wilde's, gave Kant's ideas a different colouring. Is it that the philosopher is unable to apply in detail what the artist is unable to conceive as a whole?

It is important to remember that throughout this dialogue, Wilde is speaking of pure art, a thing which possibly does not exist, and, recognising it as an ideal towards which all artists should aspire, is engaged in pointing out the more obvious means of falling short of it. He achieves a triumph, of a kind in which he delighted, by making people read of such a subject. Not wishing to be laughed at by the British intellect, and wishing to be listened to, he laughs at it instead, and, near the end of the dialogue, is so daring as to present it with a picture of what is occurring, confident that the individual will disclaim the general, and smile without annoyance at the caricature. "The stolid British intellect lies in the desert sands like the Sphinx in Flaubert's marvellous tale, and fantasy, 'La Chimère,' dances round it and calls to it with her false flute-toned voice." And the individual reader did not understand, and Wilde danced away until he felt inclined again to make him listen to the flute-toned enunciation of unfamiliar truths.

'Pen, Pencil, and Poison,' the essay on Wainewright, not in dialogue, has some of the hard angular outlines of the set article on book or public character. It fills these outlines, however, with picturesque detail and half-ironic speculation. It is impossible not to notice the resemblance between the subject of this essay and its author. It is difficult not to suspect that Wilde, in setting in clear perspective Wainewright's poisoning and writing, in estimating the possible power of crime to intensify a personality, was analysing himself, and expressing through a psychological account of another man the results of that analysis. Perhaps, in that essay we have less analysis than hypothesis. Wilde may have happened on the Life of Wainewright, and taken it, among all the books he had read, as a kind of Virgilian omen. My metaphor, as Dr. Chasuble would say, is drawn from Virgil. It used to be customary among those who wished to look into the future to open the works of that poet and to observe the lines covered by the thumb: "which lines, if in any way applicable to one's condition, were accounted prophetic." I think it possible that Wilde looked upon the little account of Wainewright that gave him a basis for his article as just such a prophetic intimation. He may have written the article to taste his future before the fact. Anyhow, he foreshadows the line of defence to be taken by his own apologists when he exclaims that "the fact of a man being a poisoner is nothing against his prose." In any discussion of the influence that Wilde's disease or crime exerted on his art, this essay would be a valuable piece of evidence. But in other things than the engaging in a secret activity, Wainewright offered Wilde a curious parallel with himself. He too introduced a new manner in writing by a new manner in dress, and Wilde was able to use his own emotions in the presence of blue china to vitalize the piece of Dutch painting, a Gabriel Metsu or a Jan van Eyck, in which he paints Wainewright with his cats, his curiosities, his crucifixes, his rare books, his cameos, and his "brown-biscuit teapots, filigree worked," against a background in which green predominates. "He had that curious love of green, which in individuals is always the sign of a subtle artistic temperament, and in nations is said to denote a laxity, if not a decadence of morals." Wilde also was fond of green. I have not counted occasions, but I have the impression that green is the colour most often mentioned alike in his verse and in his prose. Green and jade: these are his keynotes in colour, unless I am mistaken, and in these matters impressions are less likely to err than mathematics.

But the most striking and beautiful thing in *Intentions* is that dialogue between the two young men in a library whose windows look over the kaleidoscopic swirl of Piccadilly to the trees and lawns of the Green Park. They talk through the summer night, supping delicately on ortolans and Chambertin, and, in the early morning, draw the curtains, see the silver ribbon of the road, the purple mist among the trees, and walk down to Covent Garden to look at the roses that have come in from the country. There is something of Boccaccio in that setting, something, too, of Landor in the lucid sentences of their talk, and something of Walter Pater in the choice of the fruit they so idly pluck from the tree of knowledge. But Pater could not have let their conversation change so easily from smooth to ripple and from ripple to smooth; Landor would have caught the ripples and carved them in transparent moonstone, and Boccaccio would have given them girls to talk of, instead of 'The Critic as Artist.'

That would seem to be a question for the

learned and not for two young exquisites with a taste for music and books and an æsthetic dislike of the German language. But the only critical dialogue in English literature that is at all comparable with Wilde's is "The Impartial Critick" of John Dennis, who was ready to prove that choruses were unnecessary in tragedy, that Wycherley excelled Plautus, and that Shakespeare himself was not so bad as Thomas Rymer had painted him. And there too we have young men, not themselves authors, talking for pleasure's sake, drinking with discretion, now in their lodgings, now at The Old Devil and now at The Cock, reading aloud to each other and commenting verse by verse on Mr. Waller, whom they admit to be "a great Genius and a gallant Writer." There is a delightful savour about that dialogue, dry as some of the questions were that those two young sparks discussed with such wet throats. There is a suggestion of the town outside and the country beyond, of stage-coaches passing through the Haymarket, and of Hampshire gentlemen "being forbid by the perpetual Rains to follow the daily labour of their Country Sports," handing about their

Brimmers within doors, "as fast as if they had done it for Exercise." And those young men talk with just the fine superiority of Ernest and Gilbert to the authordom whose rules and persons they amuse themselves by discussing.

Ernest and Gilbert are, however, better talkers. In fact, their talk is far too good really to have been heard. They set their excellence as a barrier between themselves and life. Not for a moment will they forget that they are the creatures of art: not for a moment will they leave that calm air for the dust and turmoil of human argument. Wilde was never so sure of his art as in this dialogue, where Ernest, that ethereal Sancho Panza, and Gilbert, that rather languid Don Quixote, tilt for their hearer's joy. They share the power of visualization that made Wilde's own talk like a continuous fairy tale. They turn their ideas into a coloured pageantry, and all the gods of Greece and characters of art are ready to grace by their visible presence the exposition, whether of the ideas that are to be confuted or of those that are to take their place. "In the best days of art," says Ernest, "there were no art critics," and four pages follow in which the sculptor releases the sleeping figures from the marble, Phædrus bathes his feet in the nymph-haunted meadow, the little figures of Tanagra are shaped with bone or wooden tool from river clay, Artemis and her hounds are cut upon a veined sardonyx, the wanderings of Odysseus are stained upon the plaster, and round the earthen wine-jar Bacchus dances and Silenus sprawls.

"But no," says Gilbert, "the Greeks were a nation of art-critics." He balances with a sequence of ideas his friend's pageant of pictures. The Greeks criticized language, and "Words have not merely music as sweet as that of viol and lute, colour as rich and vivid as any that makes lovely for us the canvas of the Venetian or the Spaniard, and plastic form no less sure and certain than that which reveals itself in marble or in bronze, but thought and passion and spirituality are theirs also, are theirs indeed alone. If the Greeks had criticized nothing but language, they would still have been the great art-critics of the world. To know the principles of the highest art is to know the principles of all the arts." And so the talk goes on. There is but one defect in this panoramic method of presenting ideas. Each time that Wilde empties, or seems to spill before us, his wonderful cornucopia of coloured imagery, he seems to build a wave that towers like the blue and silver billow of Hokusai's print. Now, surely, it will break, we say, and are tempted to echo Cyril in 'The Decay of Lying,' when, at the close of one of these miraculous paragraphs, he remarks, "I like that. I can see it. Is that the end?" Too many of Wilde's paragraphs are perorations.

It is easy, in remembering the colour and rhythm of this dialogue, to forget the subtlety of its construction, the richness of its matter, and the care that Wilde brought to the consideration of his subject. I have pleased myself by working out a scheme of its contents, such as Wilde may have used in building it. Perhaps I could have found no better method of illustrating the qualities I have mentioned.

He begins with a story in the memoirs of an Academician, and, without telling it, goes on to praise autobiographies and biographies and egotism, in order to induce a frame of mind in the reader that shall make him ready to consider without too much hostility a peculiarly subjective form of art. He winds into his subject like a serpent, as Goldsmith said of Burke, by way of music, returning to the story told by the Academician, which is allowed to suggest a remark on the uselessness of art-criticism. The ideas follow in some such order as this. Bad Criticism. The Browning Society as an example. Browning. A swift and skilful return to the point at issue. The Greeks not art critics. The Greeks a nation of art critics. Life and Literature the highest arts. Walter Pater. Greek criticism of language and the test of the spoken word. Blind Milton writing by ear alone. Example of Greek criticism in Aristotle's "Poetics." Identification of the creative and critical faculties. All fine art is self-conscious. Criticism as such more difficult than creation. Action and reverie. Sin an element of progress, because it intensifies the individuality. The world made by the singer for the dreamer. Criticism itself art, a form of autobiography concerned with thoughts not events. Criticism purely subjective, and so independent of obvious subject. For examples, Ruskin's prose independent of his views on Turner; Pater's description of

Mona Lisa independent of the intention of Leonardo. "The meaning of a beautiful created thing is as much in the soul of him who looks at it, as it was in his soul who wrought it." Music. "Beauty has as many meanings as man has moods." The highest criticism " criticizes not merely the individual work of art, but Beauty itself, and fills with wonder a form which the artist may have left void, or not understood, or understood incompletely." A work of art is to the critic a suggestion for a new work of his own. Modern painting. Too intelligible pictures do not challenge the critic. Imitation and suggestion. "The æsthetic critic rejects those obvious modes of art that have but one message to deliver, and having delivered it become dumb and sterile." At this point, supper, with a promise to discuss the critic as interpreter. Part II picks up the discussion and continues. Works of art need interpretation. A true appreciation of Milton, for example, impossible without scholarship. But the truth of a critic's interpretation depends on the intensity of his own personality. All arts have their critics. The actor a critic of the drama. The executant a critic of the composer. Critics "will be always showing us the work of art in some new relation to our age." Tendency towards finding experience in art rather than in life. Life a failure from the artistic point of view, if only because a moment of life can never be lived again, whereas in literature, one can be sure of finding the particular emotion for which one looks. A pageantry of the things that have been happening in Dante for six hundred years. Baudelaire and others. The transference of emotion. Not through life but through art can we realize perfection. The immorality of art. "For emotion for the sake of emotion is the aim of art, and emotion for the sake of action is the aim of life, and of that practical organization of life that we call society." A further comparison between action and contemplation. Ernest asks, "We exist, then, to do nothing," and Gilbert answers, "It is to do nothing that the elect exist." There follows one of the few passages that contains any outspoken mention of a decadence. (This word was freely used as a label in England and France at this time.) "But we who are born at the close of this wonderful age are at once too cultured and too critical, too intellectually subtle and too curious of exquisite pleasures, to accept any speculations about life in exchange for life itself." "In the development of the critical spirit we shall be able to realise, not merely our own lives, but the collective life of the race." Heredity, "the only one of the gods whose real name we know," brings gifts of strange temperaments and impossible desires, and the power of living a thousand lives. Imagination is "concentrated race-experience." Being and becoming compared with doing. Defence of egotism. "The sure way of knowing nothing about life is to try to make oneself useful." Schoolmasters. Self-culture, not the culture of others, the proper aim of man. The idea is dangerous: so are all ideas. Ernest suggests that the fact that a critical work is subjective places it below the greatest work, which is impersonal and objective. Gilbert replies that "the difference between objective and subjective work is one of external form merely. It is accidental, not essential. All artistic creation is absolutely subjective." Critics not even limited to the more obviously subjective forms of expression, but may use drama, dialogues, narrative, or poetry. He then turns more particularly to the critic's qualifications. He must not be fair, not be rational, not be sincere, except in his devotion to the principle of beauty. Journalism, reviewing, and prurience. Intrusion of morals into art. Further consideration of the critic's qualifications. Temperament, its cultivation through decorative art. A digression on modern painting, returning to the subject of decorative art. The influence of the critic should be the mere fact of his existence. "You must not ask of him to have any aim other than the perfecting of himself." It is not his business to reform bad artists, who are probably quite irreclaimable. Remembering, but not alluding to Whistler's attack, he lets Ernest ask, "But may it not be that the poet is the best judge of poetry, and the painter of painting?" Gilbert replies, "The appeal of all art is simply to the artistic temperament." Great artists unable to recognize the beauty of work different from their own. Examples:—Wordsworth on Keats, Shelley on Wordsworth, Byron on all three, Sophocles on Euripides, Milton on Shakespeare, Reynolds on Gainsborough. The future belongs to criticism. "The subject-matter at the disposal of creation is always diminishing, while the subject-matter of criticism increases daily." The use of criticism. It makes culture possible, makes the mind a fine instrument, "takes the cumbersome mass of creative work, and distils it into a finer essence." It recreates the past. It makes us cosmopolitan. Goethe could not hate France even during her invasion of Germany. Comparison between ethics and æsthetics. "To discern the beauty of a thing is the finest point to which we can arrive." "Creation is always behind the age. It is Criticism that leads us." A swift summary, with a graceful transition to the dawn and opening windows over Piccadilly. Such is the skeleton of thought that connects all that is said, and, disguised by a wonderful skill, makes even the transitions delightful, and remembers the main purpose again and again without ever wearying us by allowing us to be conscious of repetition.

But, forgetting these mechanics and listening to that light-hearted conversation, we become aware that we are enjoying the exposition of a point of view without an understanding of which Wilde would be unintelligible as either man or writer. It does not represent him completely; a man's points of view are as various as his moods. But with 'The Decay of Lying,' it does represent what was, perhaps, the dominant mood of his life. The dialogues overlap, but do not contradict each other. It can hardly have been chance that divided them, in *Intentions*, by 'Pen, Pencil, and Poison,' that reflects the mood directly opposite, the mood in which he delighted to see a personality express itself in clothes, in vice, in action of any kind other than the vivid inaction of art. It is more likely to have been self-knowledge. For the mood that dictated the study of Wainewright was akin to that in which he found it an astounding adventure to entertain poisonous things. "It was like feasting with panthers; the danger was half the excitement." Wilde's tragedy may be traced to the conflict between these moods, the one inviting him to life, the other to art. In either case, life or art matched its colours to seduce his temperament. The mood of the dialogues was that in which he turned, not necessarily always to writing, but to seek experience in art. In this mood he preferred, if you like to put it so, to take life at second-hand, and was happier to speak of Corot than of twilight, of Turner than of sunset. In this mood, like Vivian, he did not seek in Japanese art to know Japan, but rather to learn a new country "anywhere out of the world." Ancient Greece did not mean to him the Peloponnesian War, but the candour of Grecian statuary and the small figures of Tanagra, in the folds of whose dancing dresses, that seem always to have caught the tint of the evening sky in their terra-cotta, he found the secret of quite another country than the Greece of the historian. It was always his pleasure to begin where others had ended, and criticism rather than creation came to mean for him the delicate adventures of the intellect, such a life as was the best part of his own. And so criticism became creation for him, building its impressions into things beautiful in themselves, and transforming the life of the critic into something no less delightful than the subjects of his contemplation.

Such a theory of criticism had not been stated before his time, though there had been such critics and such criticism. The abstract usually follows the concrete, and the practice dictates the precept. Wilde had in his mind as he wrote such fine flaming things as Swinburne's study of Blake, and such slow-moving magnificent pageants as "Marius the Epicurean," in which Pater had criticized a century of manners and ideas. And, perhaps, he did not forget his own 'Pen, Pencil, and Poison,' that was "a study in green," as well as a summary of the life and talents of Janus Weathercock of The London Magazine.

Beautiful criticism had been made as long ago as when Sidney wrote of the "blind crowder," whose song moved his heart like the sound of a trumpet. But men had not known what they were doing, and made lovely things with quite another purpose. Coleridge set the key for many men's playing when he said that "the ultimate end of criticism is much more to establish the principles of writing, than to furnish rules how to pass judgments on what has been written by others; if indeed it were possible that the two could be separated." And Mr. Arthur Symons, who has in our own day made fine critical things, yet says, quite humbly, that "the aim of criticism is to distinguish what is essential in the work of a writer," and again, that "criticism is a valuation of forces." Hazlitt was no further from the truth when he wrote, in a pleasant, rather malicious article on the critics of his time, that "a genuine criticism should, as I take it, reflect the colours, the light and shade, the soul and body of a work." Criticism, as Wilde saw it, was free to do all these things, but had a further duty to itself. Hazlitt, and those who read him in his own day, thought that he was giving opinions, talking, reflecting "the soul and body of a work"; but it is for himself that we read him now, and his subjects and opinions matter little beside the gusto and the fresh wind of the chalk downs that make his essays things in themselves and fit for such criticism as he liked. Wainewright too, who learnt from Hazlitt, "deals," as Wilde saw, "with his impressions of the work as an artistic whole, and tries to translate these impressions into words, to give, as it were, the literary equivalent for its imaginative and mental effect." But he did not say so, and perhaps Walter Pater's essays were the first to make it impossible not to recognize that criticism was more than a series of judgments, opinions and ideas, necessarily subordinate to the thing criticized.

Wilde, at any rate, recognized this, and carried passive recognition into active proclamation of a new creed for critics. He gave them a new creed and a new charter, and, if he had done nothing else, would have earned a place in the history of our literature. He showed that they were free to do all they had ever attempted, to track the secret stream of inspiration to its source, to work out alike the melody and counterpoint of art, to discover its principles, to enjoy its examples, to paint portraits, to talk with their sitters, to enounce ideas, to catch the fleeting sunlight and shadow of impression. They were free to do all this, and for a creed he taught them that criticism is itself a creative art, perhaps the most creative of the arts, certainly an art to be practised with no less delicate care than that of the maker of poems, the teller of stories, the painter of pictures, the man who captures a melody, or the man who shapes a dream in stone.

My private predilections may have led me to lay too much emphasis on the main contention of 'The Critic as Artist.' I hope not, but must take this opportunity of remembering that, like 'The Decay of Lying,' this dialogue is rich in other matter than theory. Wilde never, unless in the essay on Wainewright, deliberately set himself to estimate an artist or to paint a portrait. But throughout the two dialogues are scattered fragments of vivid criticism, sometimes a little swift and careless, always subordinated as notes of colour to the prevailing scheme of the whole, but never impersonal or dull. It is impossible to read a page of *Intentions* without experiencing a delightful stimulus. It is, in my opinion, that one of Wilde's books that most nearly represents him. In nothing else that he wrote did he come so near to pouring into literature the elixir of intellectual vitality that he royally spilled over his conversation.

The fourth essay in the book is not on the high level of the others. It is more practical and less beautiful, was written earlier than the rest, and published in the year after Wilde's marriage. It is interesting, but less as a thing in itself than as an indication of the character of Wilde's knowledge of the theatre. I have therefore passed it over to the next chapter.

# VII

## THE THEATRE

THERE is a public glory in the art of the theatre, a direct and immediate applause that is nearer to the face-to-face praise and visible worship that is won by conversation than the discreet approval of readers of books. Of all the arts, that of the drama is most likely to attract the talker for talk's sake. By its means he can set his fancies moving on the boards, fling his metaphors, dressed and coloured, on a monstrous screen, and entertain a thousand listeners at once. Hazlitt never wrote a play; but his was talk with a purpose. He talked to learn, to teach, to think aloud. But Lamb, who talked for the delight of himself and his friends, tried to amuse a larger audience with " Mr. H.," and, when that play was damned, joined heartily in the hisses, for fear of being mistaken for the author. Those who conspired at the Mermaid Tavern to send brave argosies of wit trafficking on a bluer sea than ever sailed Drake's galleons were playwrights to a man. Particularly the theatre attracts those dandies among authors and talkers, for whom social means as much as artistic success— Steele, Congreve, Wilde. Congreve, like Wilde, went to Trinity College, Dublin (though he was not an Irishman), came to London with but little money, was a public character before he was twenty-five, cared as much for society as for art, grew fat with success, and became a gentleman of the world. The differences between his comedies and Wilde's are not due to different aims in writing, but only to differences in their personalities, and to the change in public taste during the two centuries that passed between "Love for Love" and *The Importance of Being Earnest*. Not until Congreve had had three plays successfully acted did he write one of which "but little . . . was prepared for that general taste which seems now to be predominant in the palates of our audience."

It is important in considering Wilde's early comedies to remember the character of the audience with which he had to contend. His was a public that asked to feel as well as to smile, a public that had grown accustomed to smile with tears in its eyes, a public that was best pleased to laugh loudly and to sob into handkerchiefs, and judged a play by the loudness of the laughs and the number of the handkerchiefs that it made necessary. He had not a Restoration audience of men and women with sharpened wits and a delight in their exercise, ready to smile and quite unready to take anything seriously except amusement. It is for that reason that he called *Lady Windermere's Fan* "A Play about a Good Woman," instead of making Mrs. Erlynne a Sylvia and punishing Lord Darlington with a marriage.

The spectacular effects of the theatre, the possibilities of delightful dialogue, the public glory, of which he was always rather greedy, drew Wilde to the writing of plays. But beside these less intimate motives he had a genuine dramatic instinct that kept him from his early youth intermittently preparing himself as a playwright. The first thing he wrote after the publication of *Poems* was a play. He took it with him to America, and on his return wrote another. With the charming braggadocio of one who was quite determined that there should be an Op. XXX. he printed Op. II. on the title-page of the private issue of *The Duchess of Padua.* His public recognition as a playwright was deferred till 1892, but after the writing of *Vera,* which, I suppose, was Op. I., he seldom ceased to observe and to plan for the stage.

The character of Wilde's study of the theatre was shown in 'The Truth of Masks,' and in the dramatic criticism that he wrote in the years immediately following his marriage. It was a study of methods and concerned no less with stage-management than with the drama. Nearly thirty years ago he made a plea for beautiful scenery, and asked for that harmony between costumier and scene-painter that has been achieved in our day by Mr. Charles Ricketts and Mr. Cayley Robinson under the management of Mr. Herbert Trench. He remarked that painted doors were superior to real ones, and pointed out that properties which need light from more than one side destroy the illumination suggested by the scene-painter's shadings. From the first his dramatic criticism was written in the wings, not from the point of view of an audience careless of means, observant only of effects. *Vera* may have been dull, and *The Duchess of Padua* unplayable, but actors, at least, shall have no fault to find in the technique of *Lady Windermere's Fan*. That play seems to me to be no more than a conscious experiment in the use of the knowledge that Wilde had sedulously worked to obtain.

There was a continuity in Wilde's interest in the theatre wholly lacking in his passing fancies for narrative or essay-writing. This, with the fact that his plays brought him his first financial success, has made it usual to consider him as a dramatist whose recreations are represented by his books. Even Mr. Symons, in his article on Wilde as "An Artist in Attitudes," finds that his plays, "the wittiest that have been seen upon the modern stage," expressed, "as it happened by accident, precisely what he himself was best able to express." I cannot help feeling that this is a little unjust to him. His most perfectly successful works, those which most exactly accomplish what they attempt, without sacrificing any part of themselves, are, perhaps, *The Importance of Being Earnest* and *Salomé*. Both these are plays. But neither of them seems to me so characteristic, so inclusive of Wilde as *Intentions, De Profundis, The Portrait of Mr. W. H.*, or even *The Picture of Dorian Gray*. His plays are wilfully limited, subordinated to an aim outside themselves, and, except in the two I have just mentioned, these limitations are not such as to justify themselves by giving freedom to the artist. Some limitations set an artist free for an achievement otherwise impossible. But the limitations of which I complain only made Wilde a little contemptuous of his work. They did not save his talent from preoccupations, but compelled it to a labour in whose success alone he could take an interest.

It is impossible not to feel that Wilde was impatient of the methods and the meanings of his first three successful plays, like a juggler, conscious of being able to toss up six balls, who is admired for tossing three. These good women, these unselfish, pseudonymous mothers, these men of wit and fashion discomfited to make a British holiday; their temptations, their sacrifices, their defeats, are not taken from any drama played in Wilde's own mind. He saw them and their adventures quite impersonally; and no good art is impersonal. Salomé kissing the pale lips of Iokanaan may once have moved him when he saw her behind the ghostly footlights of that secret theatre in which each man is his own dramatist, his own stage-manager, and his own audience. But Lady Windermere did not return to her husband for Wilde's sake, and he did not feel that Sir Robert Chiltern's future mattered either way. He cared only that an audience he despised should be relieved at her return, and that to them the career of a politician should seem to be important. Not until the production of *The Importance of Being Earnest* did he share the pleasure of the pit. I know a travelling showman who makes "enjoy" an active verb, and speaks of "enjoying the poor folk" when, for coppers, he lets them ride on merry-go-rounds, and agitate themselves in swing-boats, which offer him no manner of amusement. In just this way Wilde "enjoyed" the London audiences with his early plays. He did not enjoy them himself.

Hazlitt said of Congreve that "the workmanship overlays the materials; in Wycherley the casting of the parts and the fable are alone sufficient to ensure success." Wilde may not have read Hazlitt on "The English Comic Writers," but his earlier plays suggest a determination to "ensure success" after the manner of Wycherley, and to overlay the base material necessary for that purpose with wit's fine workmanship after the manner of Congreve. The fables, the characters, the settings, were chosen on account of their experience; all were veterans with reputations untarnished by any failure in popularity. Some were taken from the English stage, some from the French; all served as the machinery to keep an audience interested and carry Wilde's voice across the footlights. In the theatre, as in storytelling, he was not unready to work to *bouts-rimés*.

I say, to carry Wilde's voice across the footlights: that is exactly what his plays do. Those neat, polished sentences, snapping like snuff-boxes, are often taken from the books that hold what he chose to preserve of his conversation. An aphorism that has served the author of *The Soul of Man* and shone for a moment in *Dorian Gray* is given a new vitality by Lord Illingworth, and what is good enough for Lady Narborough is a little better in the mouth of Dumby. Wilde was never without the power, shared by all amateurs of genius, of using up the odds and ends from one pastime to fill out the detail of another. Doing things, like Merimée, for wagers with himself, he would make plays that should be powerful in their effect on other people, but he would reserve the right to show, even while making them, that he could do something else. He learnt from Musset, and believed, with Fortunio, that "a pun is a consolation for many ills, and a play upon words as good a way as another of playing with thoughts, actions, and people." He consoled himself for his plots by taking extraordinary liberties with them, and amused himself with quips, bons-mots, epigrams and repartee that had really nothing to do with the business in hand. Most of his witty sayings would bear transplanting from one play to another, and it is necessary to consult the book if we would remember in whose mouth they were placed. This is a very different thing from the dialogue of Congreve on the one hand or of J. M. Synge on the other. The whole arrangement in conversation, as he might appropriately have called either *Lady Windermere's Fan, An Ideal Husband*, or *A Woman of No Importance*, was very much lighter than the story that served as its excuse and sometimes rudely interrupted it. It was so sparkling, good-humoured and novel that even the audience for whom he had constructed the story forgave him for putting a brake upon its speed with this quite separate verbal entertainment.

I suppose that this forgiveness encouraged him to believe that the situations and emotional appeals he borrowed from melodrama were not necessary to his success. In *The Importance of Being Earnest* he threw them bravely overboard, and wrote a play whose very foundation was a pun. Nothing could be a better proof of the inessential nature of those tricks with which he had been making sure of his audience than the immense superiority of this play to the others. Free from the necessity of living up to any drama more serious than its conversation, it preserves a unity of feeling and of tone that sets it upon a higher level. Wit is a little heartless, a little jarring, when flashed over a crisis of conscience, even when we know that the agitated politician is only a figure cut from an illustrated paper and mounted on cardboard. And passion, whether of repentance or of indignation, is a little *outré* in a picture-gallery where Lord Illingworth has said that a well-tied tie is the first serious step in life. In those first three plays, even when Wilde makes a serious effort to get dramatic value out of, for example, Lord Illingworth's worldly wisdom, he is quite unable to disguise the fact that it is an effort and serious. Those plays are interesting, amusing, clever, what you will, but their contradictions have cost them beauty. It is not in the least surprising that *The Importance of Being Earnest*, the most trivial of the social plays, should be the only one of them that gives that peculiar exhilaration of spirit by which we recognize the beautiful. It is precisely because it is consistently trivial that it is not ugly. If only once it marred its triviality with a bruise of passion, its beauty would vanish with the blow. But it never contradicts itself, and it is worth noticing that its unity, its dovetailing of dialogue and plot, so that the one helps the other, is not achieved at the expense of the conversation, but at that of the mechanical contrivances for filling a theatre that Wilde had not at first felt sure of being able to do without. The dialogue has not been weighted to trudge with the plot; the plot has been lightened till it can fly with the wings of the dialogue. The two are become one, and the lambent laughter of this comedy is due to the radio-activity of the thing itself, and not to glow-worms incongruously stuck over its surface.

It is not easy to define the quality of that laughter. It is not uproarious enough to provide the sore throat of farce. It is not thoughtful enough to pass Meredith's test of comedy. It is not due to a sense of superior intellect, like much of Mr. Shaw's. It is the laughter of complicity. We do not laugh at but with the persons of the play. We would, if we could, abet the duplicity of Mr. Worthing, and be accessories after the fact to the Bunburying of Algernon. We would even encourage Lady Bracknell's determined statement, for we are in the secret, and we know—

> She only does it to amuse,
> Because she knows it pleases.

The simultaneous speech of Cecily and Gwendolen is no insult to our intelligence, nor do we boggle for a moment over the delightful impossibility of Lane. We are caught from the beginning by a spirit of delicate fun. We busy ourselves in the intrigues, and would on no account draw back. *The Importance of Being Earnest* is to solid comedy what filigree is to a silver bowl. We are relieved of our corporeal envelopes, and share with Wilde the pleasure of sporting in the fourth dimension.

. . . . . . .

Nothing better illustrates Wilde's extraordinary versatility than his almost simultaneous business as two entirely different dramatists. The one wrote the plays we have been discussing, the other, plays so different from these in character that it is hard to believe that they are the work of the same man. These other plays have been called "romantic," a word that hardly distinguishes them from the "romantic" comedy of *The Importance of Being Earnest.* Still, Gautier and Flaubert have made it possible to attribute to that word a flavour of the South and the East, and these plays have Southern and Eastern settings that are harmonious with their contents. There is no laughter in these plays. They are nearer to *The Duchess of Padua* than to comedy. Wilde delighted in laughter but also in a quality in emotion almost hostile to laughter, a quality that I can best describe as magnificence. In his prose books both are expressed; if his dramatic writing had been limited to the four plays that brought him success, it would have seemed that the Wilde who wrote *The Sphinx* had not been represented on the stage.

But, when he was writing *Lady Windermere's Fan*, or a little earlier, he wrote down, swiftly, as if to relieve himself, a play whose mood was at the opposite end of his range. And, while *The Importance of Being Earnest* was filling the St. James's Theatre, he was trying to finish *La Sainte Courtisane*, and had submitted to a manager the latter part of *A Florentine Tragedy*, which he had never been able to begin. When he was released from prison, he left the manuscript of the first in a cab, and did not complete the second. He had imagined, while in Reading Gaol, two other such plays as *Salomé*—*Ahab and Isabel*, and *Pharaoh*. These, unfortunately, like *The Cardinal of Arragon*, portions of which Wilde was accustomed to recite, were never written.

The non-existence and the incompleteness of these plays are explicable on other grounds than those of inclination. I think that if *Salomé* had been produced with success as soon as it was written, Wilde would very likely not have written his plays about good women and conscience-stricken men of State, or, having written one, would have written no more. It is possible that we owe *The Importance of Being Earnest* to the fact that the Censor prevented Sarah Bernhardt from playing *Salomé* at the Palace Theatre. For though Wilde had the secret of a wonderful laughter, he preferred to think of himself as a person with magnificent dreams. He would rather have been a magician than a jester. The well-dressed modern plays starved too many of his intimate desires. He was unable to clothe magnificent emotions in evening dress. But applause was necessary to him. He made sure of it by the modern plays, and had not a chance of securing it by anything else. And so there are four social comedies, and only one *Salomé*.

Of the unfinished plays, as they are printed in his works, there is little to be said. *La Sainte Courtisane* is a beautiful fragment, suggesting a story rather intellectual than emotional, but an admirable framework on which to drape a cloak of imagery. The motive is the same as that of *The Portrait of Mr. W. H.* The woman covered with jewels is converted by the hermit to the love of God, and he by her to the love of the flesh. They lose their own beliefs in imparting them, and the hermit goes to Alexandria, while the woman remains in the desert. The dialogue is of the same character as that of *Salomé*, which we shall presently discuss. We cannot tell how fine a play it might have been. *A Florentine Tragedy* is less fragmentary. As Wilde left it, it was the latter part of a play in one act in blank verse, beginning with the surprisal of the lovers by the husband. The whole of the conversation between the three had been written. To fit the play for presentation on the stage, Mr. Sturge Moore wrote a preparation for it that cannot be far different from Wilde's design, and is now printed with the rest. It is not the business of this book to consider the brilliant and vigorous poetry of Mr. Sturge Moore, though it is impossible not to remember with delight passages from many of his books, always rich in ore, and again and again melting into gold. His induction to Wilde's play is perfectly calculated. He catches the spirit of Wilde's verse, and subdues his own to agreement. His is the difficult task of so drawing Bianca's character that she shall be able without incongruity to beg the young lord to kill her husband, and, when the young lord is himself killed, to come dazed towards the merchant she had despised, with the question—

"Why
Did you not tell me you were so strong?"

and receive the answer—

"Why
Did you not tell me you were beautiful?"

Wilde's is a piece of cumulative drama that keeps up an increasing tension in the audience from the moment that the husband enters till the moment when the lover dies and those two sentences are spoken. The play resembles *The Duchess of Padua* in being unable to disguise an aloof intention, an extraneous will-power, that is perfectly hidden in the earlier *Salomé*.

It is surprising to think that *Salomé* was not written with a view to production. It was only offered to Sarah Bernhardt when she asked Wilde why he had not written a play for her. The stage-directions, I am told, set almost insoluble problems to the manager, whose ideas are limited by the conventions of the modern theatre. The final speech of Salomé is of a length that demands, if abridgment is to be avoided, a consummate actress and an audience in a state of extraordinary tension. But, since the play induces such a tension, the lack of an actress can hardly be urged as a blemish on its technique. And since, when the play is produced it is extremely successful, we can only rejoice that it has shown, if only accidentally, the inadequacy of once accepted dogmas of theatrical presentation. An appeal to the populace is not good criticism, but no badly built play can show such a record of success as *Salomé*. Mr. Ross will, I am sure, allow me to use some of the heavy fire of facts with which he answered those critics who spoke of the play as having been "dragged from obscurity" when it was produced in England in 1905. "In 1901, within a year of the author's death, it was produced in Berlin; from that moment it has held the European stage. It has run for a longer consecutive period in Germany than any play by any Englishman, not excepting Shakespeare. Its popularity has extended to all countries where it is not prohibited. It is performed throughout Europe, Asia, and America. It is played even in Yiddish."

But before discussing the play itself let me set down the facts on both sides of the mild controversy over the writing of it in French. Wilde had talked of the play for some time before he wrote it, and talked of it chiefly in Paris. Frenchmen had applauded the fragments he recited. It was to them that he wished to show it when completed. This is the reason why it shares with "Vathek" and "The Grammont Memoirs" the distinction of being a work written in French by an English speaking man of genius. It has been suggested that the language made it possible, but *La Sainte Courtisane* is enough to show that it could have been written in English. There are slight disagreements over Wilde's knowledge of French. M. André Gide says that "he knew French admirably, but pretended to have to look for the words for which he meant his listeners to wait. He had almost no accent, or at most only what it pleased him to retain to give a new and strange aspect to his words." On the other hand, M. Stuart Merrill writes of his speaking French with a fantasy that, pleasant enough in conversation, would have produced a deplorable impression in the theatre. For example, Wilde ended one of his stories with " Et puis, alors, le roi il est mouru."

These pieces of evidence must be remembered when we consider the composition of *Salomé*. Mr. Ross says: "The play was passed for press by no less a writer than Marcel Schwob, whose letter to the Paris publisher, returning the proofs and mentioning two or three slight alterations, is still in my possession. Marcel Schwob told me some years afterwards that he thought it would have spoiled the spontaneity and character of Wilde's style if he had tried to harmonize it with the diction demanded by the French Academy." M. Merrill says: " Un jour Wilde me remit son drame qu'il avait écrit très rapidement, de premier jet, en français, et me demanda d'en corriger les erreurs manifestes. Ce ne fut pas chose facile de faire accepter à Wilde toutes mes corrections. . . Je me rappelle que la plupart des tirades de ses personnages commençaient par l'explétif: *enfin!* En ai-je assez biffé, des *enfin!* Mais je m'apercus bientôt que le bon Wilde n'avait en mon gout qu'une confiance relative, et je le recommandai aux soins de Retté. Celui-ci continua mon travail de correction et d'émendation. Mais Wilde finit par se méfier de Retté autant que de moi, et ce fut Pierre Louys qui donna le dernier coup de lime au texte de *Salomé*." In comment, I shall do no more than notice that the play was written in 1891, and not published till 1893. The two stories do not necessarily contradict each other, for Marcel Schwob did not suggest that he saw the manuscript, and M. Merrill's reminiscence is concerned with *Salomé* long before it was sent to the printers.

The question is not one of any great importance. It is sufficient for our purpose to observe that the French of *Salomé*, whether as Wilde wrote it or as it survived the emendations of his friends, is very simple in construction. Salomé, daughter of Herodias, Princess of Judæa, did not use the finer subtleties of the language in which she loved Iokanaan. A perusal of Maeterlinck's " Les Sept Princesses " had taught her to use a speech whose power depends on its simplicity. She, Herod, Herodias and all their entourage, speak like children who have had a French nurse. Their speech is made of short sentences, direct assertions and negations, that run like pages beside the progress of the play. They show, these short sentences, what is happening, the more forcefully, because they are themselves aloof from it and busied with their own concerns. For example :—

"*Herode.* Qu'est-ce que cela me fait qu'elle danse ou non? Cela ne me fait rien. Je suis heureux ce soir. Je suis très heureux. Jamais je n'ai été si heureux.

*Le premier soldat.* Il a l'air sombre, le tétrarque. N'est-ce pas qu'il a l'air sombre?

*Le second soldat.* Il a l'air sombre."

The effect of the play is won by the cumulative weight of these short contradictory sentences, that fall like continual drops of water on a stone, never argue, are never loud enough to be quarrelsome, and sometimes amuse themselves by reflecting, as if in a box of mirrors, a single object in a hundred ways. The moon is translated into many moods. For the page of Herodias she is a dead woman coming from the tomb to look for dead men. Salomé's lover sees her as a little dancing princess, with yellow veil and silver feet. For Salomé she is a little piece of money, cold, chaste, a virgin. The page of Herodias sees her again as a dead woman, covering herself with a winding-sheet, and when the young Syrian dies, laments that, knowing she was seeking a dead man, he had not hidden his friend in a cavern where she could not see him. Herod finds her an hysterical woman seeking lovers everywhere, naked, and refusing to be veiled by the clouds. Herodias finds that the moon resembles the moon, and that is all. Then in the eyes of Herod she becomes red in accordance with the prophecy, and Herodias replies, jeering, "And the Kings of the Earth have fear." And finally, when Salomé is speaking to the head, when all is over but her death, Herod cries aloud that the moon should be put out with the torches and the stars, because he begins to be afraid.

The drama, reflected in these images of the moon that show the changing colours of the minds that look at her, is thrown inward, and must be read between the lines. Rather than describe the strength of an emotion, or show it in immediate action, Wilde shows what it compels its possessor to disregard. Salomé answers the question of the young Syrian with irrelevant remarks, because she is obsessed by the mole's eyes of her stepfather. When Iokanaan speaks, and the young Syrian suggests that she should go into the garden in her litter, she replies simply, "Il dit des choses monstrueuses à propos de ma mère, n'est-ce pas?" When he kills himself, on account of her words to the prophet, and falls before her feet, she does not see him. The page laments, and a soldier tells her of what has happened before her eyes:—

"*Le premier soldat.* Princesse, le jeune capitaine vient de se tuer.
*Salomé.* Laisse-moi baiser ta bouche, Iokanaan."

This is potential as opposed to kinetic drama, and expresses itself not in action, but in being unmoved by action. It is an expression of the aspiration towards purely potential speech characteristic of the French symbolists, and of all who seek "a literature in which the visible world is no longer a reality, and the unseen world no longer a dream." It was, perhaps, the fear that such drama of the mind would be impossible on the stage that made Maeterlinck write as sub-title to a book of plays, " Little Dramas for Marionettes." For the speech maps out by avoidance what is really said, and whereas some plays would lose little by being acted in dumb show, these appeal less to the eye than to the ear.

In writing *Salomé*, however, Wilde did not neglect the wonderful visual sense of the theatre that was, later, to suggest to him the appearance on the stage of Jack in mourning for his non-existent brother. He was able to see the play from the point of view of the audience, and refused no means of intensifying its effect. When Salomé is leaning over the cistern, listening for the death of Iokanaan, he does not allow the executioner to come up with the head. The man would have shared the attention of the audience, and made the head a piece of meat. Instead: " Un grand bras noir, le bras du bourreau, sort de la citerne apportant sur un bouclier d'argent la tête d'Iokanaan. Salomé la saisit. Hérode se cache le visage avec son manteau. Hérodias sourit et s'évente. Les Nazaréens s'agenouillent et commencent à prier." The head, like a dramatic moment, isolated upon the stage, compels a group of characteristic actions. Its appearance is a significant speech. The strength of the emotion in the play blinds many to the beauty without which it would be worthless. Salomé's lust, wreaking itself on dead lips because it was denied them living, is, indeed, a powerful demon to subdue to the service of beauty. And the prurient, who are most intimately moved by it, make up most of those who cannot see beyond it. But this emotion is but part of a larger harmony, which, though still more powerful, is not allowed to confuse the delicate, careful fingering of the artist. Control is never lost, and, when the play is done, when we return to it in our waking dreams, we return to that elevation only given by the beautiful, undisturbed by the vividness, the clearness with which we realise the motive of passion playing its part in that deeper motive of doom, that fills the room in which we read, or the theatre in which we listen, with the beating of the wings of the angel of death.

# VIII

## DISASTER

BEFORE the success of the plays, Wilde had been an adventurer on thin ice, exhibiting a brave superiority to fortune, but painfully conscious that his income was far smaller than that on which it was possible to live with the happy extravagance that was natural to him. He had been born with the ghost of a silver spoon in his mouth, but had never been able to materialize it. It was his right to live luxuriously, since that task was one that he was peculiarly fitted to perform. Some carelessness in the inviting of his fairy godmothers, some inattention on the part of the presiding gods, had denied him that right. When the success of the plays suddenly raised his income to several thousands of pounds a year, he lost no time in living up to and above it. Some of his extravagances were of the simplest, most childish kind.

He over-fed, like a schoolboy in a tuckshop with an unexpected sovereign in his hand. Flowers he had always worn, hansom-cabs he had always used, but now he bought the most expensive button-holes, and kept his cab waiting all day. His friendships became proportionately costly, for he denied nothing to those he liked, and some of them never forgot to ask. He hurriedly ruined himself with prosperity, like the poor man in the fairy tale, whose wish for all the gold in the world was granted by a mischievous destiny.

The success of the plays and the extravagance that it permitted placed him in so strong a light of public attention that he could do nothing in secret. He became one of those people whose celebrity lends a savour to gossip. Scandal borrowed wings from the knowledge that it had a beginning in truth. In 1889, before the maleficent flood of gold was poured upon him, he had become accustomed to indulge the vice that, openly alluded to in the days and verses of Catullus, is generally abhorred and hidden in our own. He had been in youth a runner after girls, but, as a man, he ceased to take any interest in women. In the moment of his success, when many were ready to throw themselves at his feet, one, perhaps, of the reasons of his power was his own indifference to his conquests. Many excuses have been made for him. It has been suggested, for example, that in his absorption in antiquity he allowed himself to forget that he was not living in it. But Wilde was not a scholar with a rampart of books between himself and the present. Our business here is scientific, not apologetic, and such evidence as we have shows that the vice needs none but a pathological explanation. It was a disease, a malady of the brain, not the necessary consequence of a delight in classical literature. Opulence permitted its utmost development, but did not create it. Opulence did, however, make it noticeable, and prepared the circumstances in which it was publicly punished.

Wilde had always been laughed at, and, even before the facts of his conduct were generally known, the laughter was coloured by dislike. A book that was written by a small, prehensile mind, gifted with a limber cleverness, enables us to see him through the eyes of the early nineties. This book, "The Green Carnation," is a limited but faithful caricature. Wilde was accused of having written it, but characteristically replied: "I invented that magnificent flower. But with the middle-class and mediocre book that usurps its strangely beautiful name, I have, I need hardly say, nothing whatsoever to do. The flower is a work of art. The book is not." Here, as in the matter of "Patience," he could not forgo the perversity of lending colour to other people's parodies of himself. "The Green Carnation" shows us Esmé Amarinth and a youthful patrician who models himself upon him expounding the art of being self-consciously foolish, wearing green carnations, and teaching choir-boys to sing a catch about "rose-white youth" in the presence of the widow of a strong and silent British soldier. Lady Locke thinks that England has changed, and, though fascinated by Amarinth's under-study, does not marry him, for fear her "soldier's son," a stout Jehu of the governess-cart, should learn from him a soul-destroying and effeminate love of carnations pickled in arsenic. The book is like a clever statue, brightly painted, of Britannia refusing the advances of the æsthete. The æsthete is made to look rather a fool; and so is Britannia. Such sections of the public as took pleasure in it thought Wilde a peculiarly arrogant coxcomb, a disconcerting and polished reply to the Victorian tradition of muscular manhood in which they had long been secure. They were ready to rejoice in his discomfiture, and their hostility to Wilde spread swiftly and gave a quality of triumph to the delight of all classes as soon as he was arrested.

An elaborate account of the various trials would in no way serve the purpose of this book. It is sufficient to say that on May 25, 1895, he was sentenced to two years' imprisonment with hard labour.

## IX

## DE PROFUNDIS

THE book called *De Profundis*, first published in 1905, five years after Wilde's death, is not printed as it was written, but is composed of passages from a long letter whose complete publication would be impossible in this generation. The passages were selected and put together by Mr. Robert Ross with a skill that it is impossible sufficiently to admire. The letter, a manuscript of "eighty close-written pages on twenty folio sheets," was not addressed to Mr. Ross but to another friend. It was not delivered to him, but given to Mr. Ross by Wilde, who also gave instructions as to its partial publication.

Wilde is in prison, and is at pains to realize exactly what this means to him: where he is unchanged, where he has lost, and where and how he has gained. He would draw up a profit and loss account, of the loaves that are sustenance for the body and the flowers of the white narcissus that are food for the soul, and in this way give himself courage to face the world with the knowledge that he had kept his soul alive. He will discover where he stands with regard to Christianity, and where with regard to Flaubert. A critic and artist, he will realize himself among masterpieces, and discover what is altered in the personality for whose notation he has been accustomed to use his criticism of works of art. "To the artist, expression is the only mode under which he can conceive life at all. To him what is dumb is dead."

Wilde's life in prison was lived on two planes. Only one of them is represented in *De Profundis*. In writing that letter he was able to pick up the frayed threads of his intellectual existence, to find that some were gold and some were crimson, and to learn that whatever else he might have lost he had not lost his lordship over words. The existence whose threads he thus collected was not that which was at the moment determining the further development of his character. It was an aftermath of that summer of the intellect that had given him *Intentions*. Instead of

the debonair personality of an Ernest or a
Gilbert, he painted now a no less ideal vision
of himself in circumstances similar to those
that now surrounded him.

Behind this imaginary and as it were
dramatic life was another in which he shared
the days and the day's business of his fellow
convicts.

> "We tore the tarry rope to shreds
>   With blunt and bleeding nails;
> We rubbed the doors, and scrubbed the floors
>   And cleaned the shining rails:
>   And rank by rank, we soaped the plank,
>   And clattered with the pails."

There was the routine of the prison, the daily
walk for one hour round a circular path,
watched by warders, inside a wall that hid
all but the sky and the topmost branches of
a tree, upon whose bare twigs, buds, and green
and ruddy leaves, the prisoners depended for
news of the magnificent passage of the
seasons. These daily walks, like all the work
of the prison, took place in silence, broken
only by the warders' words of command
delivered in the raucous voice that tradition
has dictated. As speech is the greatest of
man's privileges, so its deprivation is the least

bearable of his punishments. During the daily walks even those convicts who in other things are obedient to the prison discipline, learn to speak without a perceptible motion of the lips. For six weeks Wilde walked in silence, but one evening at the end of that time, he heard the man walking behind him say: " Oscar Wilde, I am sorry for you. It must be worse for you than for us." He nearly fainted, and replied: "No; it's the same for all of us." In this way he made the acquaintanceship of his fellows. One by one he talked with all of them, and these scraps of conversation, he told M. André Gide, made his life so far tolerable that he lost his first desire of killing himself. "The only humanizing influence in prison is the prisoners," he wrote after he came out. Except in the matter of permission to write (a permission not granted until near the end of his term, and then only on the recommendation of the doctor), the prison discipline was in no way relaxed for Wilde. He slept on a plank bed. He did not, like Wainewright, remain "a gentleman," and share a cell with a bricklayer and a sweep, neither of whom ever offered him the brush. He cleaned out his cell, polished his tin drinking cup, turned the crank, and picked the oakum like the rest.

Echoes of these things are heard in *De Profundis*, but if, as Wilde had, we have made ourselves

> "Misers of sound and syllable, no less
> Than Midas of his coinage,"

it is not in what books say but in their style that we look for the secrets of their writers. And it is impossible not to notice that the character of Wilde's prose in this book is not very different from that in *Intentions*. He observed changes in himself, and foresaw others, but the real alteration of his point of view was not accomplished until he came out of prison. In gaol he was in retreat, like a man who has gone into a monastery. The world was still the world that he had left, and not until he was again free did he realize more vividly than by speculation how different his life was to be, and across what a gulf he would look back at the existence that had been broken off by his disaster. His artistic attitude had not yet been changed.

It is for this reason that the book raises so easily a question dear to those who prefer praising or blaming to understanding. Is it sincere? they ask. Is it possible that a man who felt such things sincerely could write of his feelings in such mellifluous prose? Is it sincere? they ask, with particular insistence, pointing to the character of Wilde's life after leaving prison as a proof that it was not. And if not, what then? Why then, they say, it is worthless.

"Blind mouths! that scarce themselves know how to hold
A sheep-hook, or have learnt aught else the least
That to the faithful herdsman's art belongs!
What recks it them? What need they? They are sped;
And, when they list, their lean and flashy songs
Grate on their scrannel-pipes of wretched straw."

They demand that the truth shall be told in a hoarse voice, that they may recognize it, and yet the ugly, conscientious noise of their scrannel-pipes is no nearer than *De Profundis* to the sincerity they admire. Sincerity, in the sense that they give to that word, does not exist in art. "What people call insincerity is simply a method by which we can multiply our personalities." That sentence, from the mouth of one of the personalities that Wilde was able to assume, explains the obvious variety of his work. It throws also no dubious light upon the general nature of art. For in art no attitude is insincere whose result is beautiful, and no attitude is possible whose result may not be beautiful. All depends on the artist and on the depth and abandon of his insincerity. For art tolerates many contradictions, but a work of art tolerates none. The man who takes an attitude and is unable to sustain it, who smirks at the audience, who plays as it were the traitor to his own choice, can produce nothing but what is ugly, since, like him, it will contain a contradiction. But the man who chooses an attitude, and preserves it consistently in any work of art, is thereby fulfilling a condition of beauty. He may make a lovely thing, and then, taking another attitude, may contradict himself in a thing of no less loveliness. Repentance like that in *De Profundis* is a guarantee of a moment of humility, but not of a life of reform. Shakespeare wrote Hamlet's soliloquy and also Juliet's murmuring from the balcony. Yet he was not always in love, nor always melancholy with inaction. We are accustomed to insincerity in play-writing, and do not expect each character, fool or wise, young or old, to represent its author. We allow, as, for an obvious example, in Restoration comedy, plays to be written from a standpoint that their authors could not possibly maintain in private life. In poetry also, we do not consider Browning insincere because he speaks now for Lippo Lippi, and now for Andrea del Sarto. In novels we allow Fielding to write "Jonathan Wild" as a satirist, and "Joseph Andrews" as a comic romancer, and we are not shocked when he relishes in imagination deeds that as a magistrate he would be bound to censure. I think we have to learn that all fine literature is dramatic. No man pours from his mouth in any single speech all the roses and the vomit that would represent his soul. Men speak and hold their peace. They make and their hands are still. And many moods flit by while they are silent, and myriad souls agitate the blood in the veins of those motionless hands. The artist is he who, remembering this mood or that, can hold it fast and maintain it long enough for the making of a work of art. We do not ask him to retain it further. The shaping of his mood in words or in clay has already changed his personality. The writer of a mad song need not gibber in the streets. Golden phrases lose none of their magnificence if he who made them wears plain homespun when we meet him in the market-place. He has been a king for a moment, and given us his kingship for ever. We can ask no more.

Wilde, perhaps more than other men, insisted on the dramatic character of his work. In considering any of it we should remember those sentences in the last paragraph of 'The Truth of Masks':—" Not that I agree with everything that I have said in this essay. There is much with which I entirely disagree. The essay simply represents an artistic standpoint, and in æsthetic criticism attitude is everything." I am not sure that this confession does not spoil 'The Truth of Masks.' It is perilously like an aside; but Wilde was sufficiently subtle to have chosen a mood which such an aside would illustrate rather than contradict. In considering his work, we must remember, first, that all work is dramatic, true to an individual mood only; and, secondly, that Wilde, more clearly conscious of this than most artists, was better able to take advantage of it. He was freed from those qualms of conscience which made Swinburne glad to differentiate his earlier from his later works by saying:—"In my next work it should be superfluous to say that there is no touch of dramatic impersonation or imaginary emotion." This sentence, that denies together what is universal and what does not exist (since you cannot imagine an emotion without feeling it) points to no blemish in Swinburne's work, but only to a discomfort of mind that some of it must have caused him. From this discomfort Wilde was free. He had many tuning-forks, and distrusted none of them because it happened to be pitched differently from another.

There is no doubt that, when *De Profundis* was finished, Wilde regarded it as a document of historical value, as a veracious confession. This is clear from the tone in which he wrote of it to Mr. Ross:—"I don't defend my conduct. I explain it. Also there are in my letter certain passages which deal with my mental development in prison, and the inevitable evolution of my character and intellectual attitude towards life that has taken place; and I want you and others who still stand by me and have affection for me to know exactly in what mood and manner I hope to face the world." Those sentences certainly let us see the attitude that Wilde hoped to induce in his readers, but, if we would turn to Wilde himself, and, careless of the beauty of the work, pry past it to discover the private feelings of the author, we must take them not as a statement of the truth, but, seeking the truth, take that statement into account. That statement, the published *De Profundis*, those unpublished portions of the letter which, probably, will never be read in our lifetime, the whole of Wilde's works, the whole of his life, the character of that person to whom he was immediately writing, the character of those other friends by whom he desired to be read, the character which, without deliberate choice, he had himself grown accustomed to present to them: we must know all these things, and be able to weigh them exactly, and balance them justly against each other. Have I not said enough to show that it is a vain task to seek for the absolute truth in such a matter, and that we are better and more hopefully employed when we concern ourselves simply with a wonderful piece of literature dictated by certain conditions that we admit are impossible accurately to discover?

In pointing out that the details of Wilde's life in prison did not affect the manner of his thought, but only provided him with fresh material, I do not wish to suggest that prison was unimportant to him. It might have been. He might, in revolt against it, have made it no more than a hideous accident, stunting his nature by refusing to allow it to assimilate the black bread that had been thrown to it as well as the sweetened cakes. If he had been earlier released, as he said, this might have happened. He was not released, and revolt was changed to acceptance, and, at last, he was able to say, as he had hoped, that society's sending him to prison ranked with his father's sending him to Oxford, as a turning point in his life. But that is a question for the next chapter, for imprisonment did not radically alter him until he was again in the world.

In prison, however, the anæsthetic of magnificent living was denied him, and he turned to magnificent thought, recovering the power that had been his before popular success had narrowed his horizon.

## DE PROFUNDIS

" Knowing the possible, see thou try beyond it
Into impossible things, unlikely ends ;
And thou shalt find thy knowledgeable desire
Grow large as all the regions of thy soul." [1]

In 1894 he had known the possible, and achieved it in *The Importance of Being Earnest*. But in 1889 he had been trying far beyond it, and now again, in prison, he found his desires growing far beyond the possible, and covering the regions of his soul. He needed an idea that should make this bread-and-water existence one with that of wine and lilies, an idea that should make it possible for him to conceive his life as a whole, and, in the conception, make it so.

In *De Profundis* he tries to make his friend realize what he has scarcely realized himself: the depth of his fall, the twilight in his cell, the twilight in his heart, the nature of suffering, the nature of the sorrow that does not allow itself to be forgotten. He writes passages so poignant as to blind us to their beauty, for sorrow is no less sorrow when it walks in purple than when in rags it lies in the dust. Then, after showing the ruins of his life, he paints a picture, no less

[1] From "The Sale of St. Thomas." By Lascelles Abercrombie.

poignant, of himself rebuilding that broken edifice with those things that he has hitherto rejected. He has learnt, he tells himself, the value of pain and the virtue of humility. He has once believed that pain was a blemish on creation, and that the sobbing of a child made the gods hide their faces for shame. He now believes that suffering is a means for the purification of the spirit, a fire through which vessels of clay must pass to their perfection. And, for humility, he discovers that there is no defiance so lofty as that of self-accusation. He has been told to forget who he is; life in prison almost compels him to rebellion; but he has learnt that only by remembering his identity, by shifting to his own shoulders the burden of his disaster, and by an absolute acceptance of all that has happened in and to him, will he be able to win the pride that humility confers and that rebellion makes impossible.

This purpose, to give his life the unity he demanded from a poem; these motives, of suffering and humility, run waveringly through *De Profundis*, carrying with them here and there fragments of mournful experience. Through them he came to contemplate

Christ, not only as a type of humility and suffering, but also as an example of one whose life was a work of art. In such books as *De Profundis*, the continuous wandering speech of a mind following itself, some paragraphs seem to withdraw themselves a little, as the keynotes of the rest. Such paragraphs are, I think, those in which he wrote of Christ as the supreme artist, of Christ's influence on art, and of his philosophy as Wilde interpreted it. These paragraphs have seemed blasphemous to some and unreasonable to others. I cannot consider them more blasphemous than a Madonna and Child by Murillo, or a Christ and his Father by Milton, or more unreasonable than those persons who are unable to perceive that religion, no less than the Sabbath, was made for man, and not for the delectation of the Almighty.

Man makes God in his own image, or as he would like himself to be, and, as man's image changes, so is his God continually recast. Wilde's prose-poem of the artist and the bronze is the story of the making and remaking of religion. The Christ of the Roman slaves who escaped from their masters' rods to worship their God in cellars was indeed a Man of Sorrows, who found in misery and low estate the means of creating loveliness. As they hoped, he promised, and each labourer's penny was minted with the superscription he had himself designed. With the renaissance of joy came new Christs. One taught the Irish monks to build their wattled cells. Another, delighting in richness no less than in simplicity, designed the stone lacework of the French cathedrals. Later, the sombre, fiery Calvin saw a divinity of black and scarlet. Milton's God conceived humanity as an epic, whose conclusion must neither be hurried nor delayed. There have been Gods of war and Gods of peace, changing with man's desires. It is for that reason that we are warned to make no graven images, lest we should commit ourselves to a God of a single mood. It was quite natural that the Christ whom Wilde saw, as he sat on the wooden bench in his cell and turned the pages of his Greek Testament, should be a Christ who showed that in all the acts of his life there had been hope, a Christ who perceived "the enormous importance of living completely for the moment," swept aside the tyranny of orthodoxy, and "regarded sin and suffering as being in themselves beautiful holy things and modes of perfection."

Wilde expresses his conception with incomparable wit and charm. When he speaks of Christ's love of the sinner, he remarks that "the conversion of a publican into a Pharisee would not have seemed to him a great achievement." On Christ's view that " one should not bother too much over affairs," he comments, "the birds didn't, why should man?" And again : "The beggar goes to heaven because he has been unhappy. I cannot conceive a better reason for his being sent there. The people who work for an hour in the vineyard in the cool of the evening receive just as much reward as those who have toiled there all day long in the hot sun. Why shouldn't they? Probably no one deserved anything." And I cannot refrain from reminding myself by writing it down, of his beautiful comparison of the Greek Testament with the version that endless repetition without choice of occasion has made an empty noise in our ears : "When one returns to the Greek, it is like going into a garden of lilies out of some narrow and dark house." It pleased him to accept the not generally received view of some scholars, that Greek was the language actually spoken by Christ, and that τετελεσται [1] was indeed his last word and not a mere translation of a similar expression in a Nazarene dialect of Aramaic.

But Wilde's study of the gospels had left him more than a handful of phrases, and these chance flowers must not blind us to the garden of thought in which they grew. Among the subjects on which he planned to write was "Christ as the precursor of the romantic movement in life." This essay was never written, but Wilde had made it almost unnecessary by those suggestive paragraphs in the letter to his friend.

Christ, for him, was a supreme artist, who chose to build a beautiful thing in life instead of in marble or song. Marble and song are to the artist means of living, indeed the medium of the highest life of which he is capable. Christ essayed the more difficult task of giving life itself the unity and the loveliness that another might have given stone or melody. And this beautiful and complete life, more moving in its completeness than that of any of the gods of Greece, who " in spite of the

[1] ΚΑΤΑ ΙΩΑΝΝΗΝ, XIX, 30.

white and red of their fair fleet limbs were
not really what they appeared to be," was at
once a work of art and the life of an artist.
Christ, Wilde saw, cared more for intensity
than for magnificence, for the soul more than
raiment. His teaching was not one of the
refusal of experience, but of self-development.
He set personality above possessions, and
told his followers to forgive their enemies,
for their own sake, not because their enemies
wished to be forgiven; it is very annoying to be
forgiven. " But," says Wilde, "while Christ
did not say to men ' Live for others,' he pointed
out that there was no difference at all between
the lives of others and one's own life." And
it is this truth that marks the difference between ancient and modern art. In reading
ancient critics of ancient art, we perceive that
their view of the tragedies whose performance
they were privileged to see in the open amphi-
theatres of Greece was narrower than ours.
Theirs was the spectacle of a good man or a
good woman at odds with tragic circumstance.
We have made tragic circumstance human,
and, though we walk with Christ to Calvary, we
also wash trembling hands with Pontius Pilate.

It is just this widened sympathy, this vitalization of other things in a story besides the hero, that divides what is called romantic from what is called classical art. To Greek tragedy there was a background of the Fates; but nobody sympathized with them. In whatever is classical as opposed to romantic in modern art, we shall find a background of Fates with whom nobody sympathizes, in whom nobody believes. But all the world was alive to St. Francis. Shakespeare is myriad-mouthed as well as myriad-minded. Daffodils are alive for him no less than kings, and Iago is a man no less than Othello. And in all art that springs from the spirit, thought Wilde, "wherever there is a romantic movement in art, there somehow, and under some form, is Christ, or the soul of Christ." Wilde, thinking in prison of Christianity in art, saw through the stone walls the cathedral at Chartres in the blue morning mist, Dante and Virgil walking in hell, the painted ship of the ancient mariner idly rocking upon the painted ocean, Juliet leaning from her balcony, Pierre Vidal flying as a wolf before the hounds, the irises of Baudelaire, the bird-song of Verlaine, the breaking heart of Russian storytelling, Tannhäuser in the Venusberg, and all the flowers and children who have laughed in a wind of song.

For the mind, as for love,

> "Stone walls do not a prison make,
> Nor iron bars a cage."

Wilde had all the art of the world before him as he wrote. Seldom in his life did his thought move more magnificently and with greater wealth of illustration than in the cell where, in a perpetual twilight, his mind alone could illumine itself, and in its own light pursue that game of thinking whose essential it is to be free and harmonious.[1] Its harmonies are those of agreement with its own character, like the harmonies of art. Its freedom is that of the consistent representation of the character chosen by the thinker. In *De Profundis* Wilde wrote as harmoniously and freely as if his life were spent in conversation instead of in silence, in looking at books and pictures instead of in shredding oakum or in swinging the handle of a crank.

It is impossible too firmly to emphasize the

---

[1] "L'exercice de la pensée est un jeu, mais il faut que ce jeu soit libre et harmonieux."—REMY DE GOURMONT.

division between the texture of the life in *De Profundis* and that of Wilde's life in prison, a division not only needing explanation but explicable in the light of later events. When he left prison he wrote *The Ballad of Reading Gaol*. Now that ballad would have been obscured or enriched by a silver cobweb of scarcely perceptible sensations if it had been written before or during his imprisonment. Wilde could not then have suffered some of the harsh and crude effects that are harmonious with its character and necessary to its success. The newly-learnt insensibility, that allowed him to use in the ballad emotions that once he would have carefully guarded himself from perceiving, had been taught him in prison. In prison his nerves had been so jangled that they responded only to a violent agitation, so jarred that a delicate touch left them silent. But at the time of the writing of *De Profundis* these janglings and jarrings were too immediate to affect him. They disappeared like print held too close to the eye. He escaped from them as he wrote, for he wrote from memory. While the events were happening, had just happened, and might happen again, that produced the insensibility without which he could not have secured the broad and violent effects of his later work, he returned, in writing, to an earlier life. When he took up his pen, it was as if none of these things were, unless as material for the use of an aloof and conscious artist. He was outside the prison as he wrote, and only saw as if in vision the tall man, with roughened hands, who had once been " King of life," and now was writing in a cell.

## X

### 1897-1900

"All trials," wrote Wilde, "are trials for one's life, just as all sentences are sentences of death; and three times have I been tried. The first time I left the box to be arrested, the second time to be led back to the house of detention, the third time to pass into a prison for two years. Society, as we have constituted it, will have no place for me, has none to offer; but Nature, whose sweet rains fall on unjust and just alike, will have clefts in the rocks where I may hide, and secret valleys in whose silence I may weep undisturbed. She will hang the night with stars so that I may walk abroad in the darkness without stumbling, and send the wind over my footprints so that none may track me to my hurt: she will cleanse me in great waters, and with bitter herbs make me whole."

He asked too much, both from Nature and

from himself. Society would indeed have none of him, as he had foreseen, but Nature could only harbour for a moment this liver in great cities who had told her that her use was to illustrate quotations from the poets, and had said that he preferred to have her captive on his walls in the canvases of Corot and of Constable, than to live in her cruder landscapes. He had never intended to make too elaborate an advance to her. He had learnt from Stevenson's letters that that ingenious man had "merely extended the sphere of the artificial by taking to digging." He knew that reading Baudelaire in a café would be more natural to him than an agricultural existence. He was determined, however, not to return to the extravagances of his life before prison, and he hoped that the country would help him to keep this resolve. He was to learn that "one merely wanders round and round within the circle of one's personality." When he left prison he did not know that one must keep moving, but hoped to choose a pleasant point in his personality, and stay there.

Released from prison on May 19, 1897, he crossed the Channel to Dieppe, where he stayed for some days, and drove about with Mr. Robert Ross and Mr. Reginald Turner, examining the surrounding villages, most of which seemed uninhabitable. At the end of a week he took rooms in the inn at the little hamlet of Berneval.

Here, for the first time, he lost his power of turning life into tapestry. Alone in his cell he had written the magnificent pageant of *De Profundis*, a pageant of purple and fine linen, though he who wrote it wore the coarse cloth of convict dress. Set suddenly in the world again, he was cut off more sharply from his former existence than ever he had been cut off in prison. He became blithe and smiling, like a child who has had no past. He bathed, and was amused at the simplicity of his experience, which he laughingly attributed to having attended Mass and so not bathing as a pagan. . . . " I was not tempted by either Sirens or Mermaidens, or any of the green-haired following of Glaucus. I really think this is a remarkable thing. In my Neronian days the sea was always full of Tritons blowing conches, and other unpleasant things. Now it is quite different." " Prison has completely changed me," he said to

M. André Gide, who visited him at Berneval; "I counted on it for that." He spoke with disparagement of a man who urged him to take up his former life, a thing, he said, which one must never do. "Ma vie est comme un œuvre d'art; un artiste ne recommence jamais deux fois la même chose . . . ou bien c'est qu'il n'avait pas réussi. Ma vie d'avant la prison a été aussi réussie que possible. Maintenant c'est une chose achevée." He felt that a continuation of a life that had, as it were, ended in prison, would be like adding a sixth act and a happy ending to a tragedy, a deed repulsive to an artist, who finds it hard enough to bear when murdered Cæsar doffs his wig and smiles upon the audience that has witnessed the agony of his death. He did not wish to appear in Paris until he had had time to lay aside the costume he had worn in the play that, he was glad to think, was now concluded. He did not wish to be received as a released convict, but as the author of a new work of art. "If I can produce only one beautiful work of art I shall be able to rob malice of its venom, and cowardice of its sneer, and to pluck out the tongue of scorn by the roots."

For the moment, at any rate, he was content in the country, and asked M. Gide to send him a Life of St. Francis.

"If I live in Paris," he wrote, "I may be doomed to things I don't desire. I am afraid of big towns. Here I get up at 7.30. . . . I am happy all day. I go to bed at 10 o'clock. I am frightened of Paris . . . I want to live here." He visited the little chapel of Notre Dame de Liesse, and persuaded the curé to celebrate Mass there. He made friends with a farmer and urged him to adopt three children. He found that the customs-officers were bored, and lent them the novels of Dumas père. And on the day of the Queen's Diamond Jubilee he entertained forty children from the school with their master so successfully that for days after they cheered when he passed: "Vive Monsieur Melmoth[1] et la Reine d'Angleterre." In his first enthusiasm for Berneval he wished to build a house there, and did, indeed, take a châlet for the season, giving Mr. Ross, through whom his allowance passed, all sorts of amusing reasons for doing so, and for hurrying on the necessary preliminaries.

[1] After he left prison he took the name of Sebastian Melmoth.

He planned the arrangement of the house with something of the impatient delight of a student furnishing his first independent rooms. He asked for his pictures, and for Japanese gold paper that should provide a fitting background for lithographs by Rothenstein and Shannon. The Châlet Bourgeat was ready for habitation on June 21. A month later he wrote of *The Ballad of Reading Gaol:* "The poem is nearly finished. Some of the verses are awfully good."

Soon afterwards he changed his plans and went from Berneval to Naples.

. . . . . . .

I have particularly noticed the change in his mental attitude that became apparent at Berneval, because I think that it throws light on the character of the work he did after leaving prison, so markedly different from that of *De Profundis,* or *Intentions,* or *The Sphinx,* or any other of the delightful designs it had pleased him to embroider. What is remarkable in *The Ballad of Reading Gaol,* apart from its strength, or its violence of emotion, is a change in the quality of Wilde's language. A distinction between **decoration** and realism, though it immediately suggests itself, is too blunt to enable us to state clearly a change in Wilde's writing that it is impossible to overlook. We require a more sensitive instrument, and must seek it in a definition of literature, a formula that is concerned with the actual medium that literature employs.

To make such a definition I have borrowed two words from the terminology of physical science. Energy is described by physicists as kinetic and potential. Kinetic energy is force actually exerted. Potential energy is force that a body is in a position to exert. Applying these terms to language, without attempting too strict an analogy, I wish to define the medium of literature as a combination of kinetic with potential speech. There is no such thing in literature as speech purely kinetic or purely potential. Purely kinetic speech is prose, not good prose, not literature, but colourless prose, prose without atmosphere, the sort of prose that M. Jourdain discovered he had been speaking all his life. It says things. An example of purely potential speech may be found in music. I do not think it can be made with words, though we can give our minds a taste of it in listening to a meaningless but narcotic incantation, or a poem in a language that we do not understand. The proportion between kinetic and potential speech and the energy of the combination vary with different poems and with the poetry of different ages.

Let me take an example of fine poetry, and show that it does perform in itself this dual function of language. Let us examine the first stanza of Blake's "The Tiger":—

> "Tiger! Tiger! burning bright
> In the forests of the night,
> What immortal hand or eye
> Could frame thy fearful symmetry?"

It is impossible to deny the power of suggestion wielded by those four lines, a power utterly disproportionate to what is actually said. The kinetic base of that stanza is only the proposition to a supposed tiger of a difficult problem in metaphysics. But above, below, and on either side of that question, completely enveloping it, is the phosphorescence of another speech, that we cannot so easily overhear.[1]

[1] For a longer but still inadequate discussion of the question, see an article in my "Portraits and Speculations." Macmillan, 1913.

Let me now apply this formula of kinetic and potential speech to a definition of the change in Wilde's aims as a writer, that is illustrated by *The Ballad of Reading Gaol.* I have said that the proportion between kinetic and potential speech varies with different poems and the poetry of different ages. The poets of the eighteenth century, for example, cared greatly for kinetic speech, though the white fire of their better work shows that they were fortunately prevented from its invariable achievement. The Symbolists of the nineteenth century cared greatly for potential speech. "Nommer un objet," said Mallarmé, "c'est supprimer les trois quarts de la jouissance du poème qui est faite du bonheur de deviner peu à peu. Le suggérer, voilà le rêve." Mallarmé, indeed, went so far as to work over a poem, destroying where he could its kinetic speech, its direct statement, in the effort to make it purely potential. He is not intelligible, except where he failed in this. Wilde grew up with the Symbolists, and under the influence of the Pre-Raphaelites. His criticism of pictures accurately reflects his aims as a writer. The critic, he says, will turn from pictures that are too intelligible, that "do not stir the imagination but set definite bounds to it"; "he will turn from them to such works as make him brood and dream and fancy, to works that possess the subtle quality of suggestion, and seem to tell us that even from them there is an escape into a wider world." He will have none of "those obvious modes of art that have but one message to deliver, and having delivered it become dumb and sterile." He recognised suggestion or, as I prefer to say, potentiality, in pictures that were decorations rather than anecdotes, and, in his preference of potential over kinetic speech, made his own work decorative rather than realistic. Decoration was for him a mode of potentiality. Like the Symbolists, he had a sort of contempt for kinetic speech, because while it obviously preponderates in the kind of writing that he considered bad, he did not perceive that it is also essential in the writing that he admitted to be good. This view was intimately connected with his character, and before he could write a poem whose kinetic was comparable to its potential power he had to change completely his attitude towards life. He could not, without doing violence to himself, have written *The Ballad of Reading Gaol* before his imprisonment.

Such an alteration in his attitude became apparent when he was released : not before. And he then proceeded to write a poem whose potentiality was not won at the expense of directness. The difference between the work he did before and after his release is the same, though not so exaggerated, as that between Mallarmé and the eighteenth-century poets. The later work falls midway between these two extremes. It is writing that depends, far more nearly than anything he had yet done in verse, upon its actual statements. *The Ballad of Reading Gaol* is not more powerfully suggestive than *The Sphinx*, but what it says, its translatable element, is more important to its effect than the catalogue of the Sphinx's lovers.

We can more accurately observe this change of attitude if we examine the early version of the ballad. This version, as it is now printed by the side of that originally published, represents the poem as it was when Wilde wrote to say that it was nearly finished. It is probably very like what the poem would have been if he had not broken short his stay at

Berneval. The momentary retaste of his former life at Naples gave him the more decorative verses that were then added, and the contrast between the two moods made possible his disregard of the beliefs he once had held concerning the evil effect of a message on a work of art. At the same time, he realized at Naples how far he had departed from his old standards, and added a certain recklessness to his already altered equipment. For example, he had written at Berneval one stanza of direct statement that he had afterwards deleted with others from the first version that he sent to England:—

> "The Governor was strong upon
> The Regulation Act:
> The Doctor said that Death was but
> A scientific fact:
> And twice a day the Chaplain called
> And left a little tract."

At Naples he replaced it. He admits, in a letter to Mr. Ross, that "the poetry is not good," and says, "I have put 'The Governor was strict upon the Regulation Act'—I now think that strong is better. The verse is meant to be colloquial—G. R. Sims at best—and when one is going for a coarse effect, one had better be coarse. So please restore 'strong.'" I think that nothing could more clearly illustrate the difference between Wilde as artist before and after he was released. The change was radical, and appeared not only in the medium of his work but in its intention. He had once said that nothing was sadder in the history of literature than the career of Charles Reade, who, after writing "The Cloister and the Hearth," "wasted the rest of his life in a foolish attempt to be modern, to draw public attention to the state of our convict prisons." Now, he cheerfully labelled his ballad, "Poetry and Propaganda," and admitted that though the poem should end with the fifth canto, he had something to say and must therefore go on a little longer. He had once written for his own admiration, and, to his disadvantage, for that of people he might meet at dinner. He now wished to publish his ballad in one of the more widely read newspapers, to reach the sort of people who had shared his life in gaol. He had become anxious to speak and to be heard, and was no longer content to make and to be admired.

Little trace of the friction of change is left

in the poem. It is true that in certain lights a reader may perceive that he is examining a palimpsest, and wonder what manner of writer he was whose writing is obliterated. But there is an energy in the ballad that swings even the more obvious propaganda into the powerful motion of the poetry. Nowhere else in Wilde's work is there such a feeling of tense muscles, of difficult, because passionate, articulation. And this was the effect that he was willing to achieve. The blemishes on the poem, its moments of bad verse, its metaphors only half conceived (like the filling of an urn that has long been broken) scarcely mar the impression. It is felt that a relaxed watchfulness is due to the effort of reticence. I know of no other poem that so intensifies our horror of mortality. Beside it Wordsworth's sonnets on Capital Punishment debate with aloof, respectable philosophy the expediency of taking blood for blood, and suggest the palliatives with which a tender heart may soothe the pain of its acquiescence. Even Villon, who, like Wilde, had been in prison, and, unlike Wilde, had been himself under sentence of death, is infinitely less actual. He sees only after death: the gibbet, the row of corpses, their heads hanging, the eyes picked from their sockets by the crows, a row of blackened, sun-dried bodies swinging in wind and rain. He sees that, and thinks it a pitiful spectacle, but his only prayer is "qu'enfer n'ayt de nous la maistrie!" For Wilde it is life that matters. After it, who knows? A pall of burning lime, a barren spot where might be roses. But he lives an hundred times life's last moments, and multiplies the agony of the man who dies in the hearts of all those others who feel with him how frail is their own perilous hold.

. . . . . .

Wilde's two letters to The Daily Chronicle, 'On the Case of Warder Martin,' and 'On Prison Reform,' show just such a change in his attitude towards social questions as that which the ballad shows in his attitude towards poetry. I have not, so far, said anything of *The Soul of Man under Socialism*, and I left undiscussed the consciousness of social problems that is apparent in some of the fairy tales. It seemed better to consider these things later in the book, when it should be possible to compare his attitudes towards the social system before and after he had come in conflict with it.

At the beginning of his career he had written republican poetry, but had prefaced it with the avowal :—

"Not that I love thy children, whose dull eyes
See nothing save their own unlovely woe,
Whose minds know nothing, nothing care to know,—
But that the roar of thy Democracies,
Thy reigns of Terror, thy great Anarchies,
Mirror my wildest passions like the sea
And give my rage a brother——!"

But for this, he says, nations might be wronged and he remain unmoved,

"   .   .   .   and yet, and yet,
These Christs that die upon the barricades,
God knows it I am with them, in some things."

For several years this double attitude persisted, though, as Wilde left boyhood he left also the rage and the passions, if he had ever had them, that could only be mirrored by turbulent oceans and fiery revolutions. He was, however, increasingly troubled by the knowledge that he could not accept the comfortable belief of Dr. Pangloss, that this is the best of all possible worlds. If he had lived among the poor, he would, perhaps, have amused them by pointing out the undeserved misery of the rich. As he happened, mostly, to live among the rich, he stimulated their enjoyment of their position by reminding them of the insecurity of their tenure, of the existence of the poor, and of the inadequacy of the means adopted to eliminate them. At that time in England many charitable movements, now institutions, had only lately started upon their curious careers, and, as Wilde pointed out, men "tried to solve the problem of poverty, for instance, by keeping the poor alive; or, in the case of a very advanced school, by amusing the poor." Wilde suggested no remedies, but used his own clear perception of the difficulty, and the uneasiness of other people's minds, as a background for much delightful conversation, and for such stories as that of 'The Young King,' who sees in dreams the pain that is hidden in the pearl that the diver has brought for his sceptre, the toil woven into the golden tissues of his robes, and the blood that fills with light the rubies of his crown.

Yet Wilde was not without a personal stake in the solution of the problem, for, though he lived among the rich, he was himself one of the poor. He had not had enough money to write as he pleased and when he pleased. He had had to lecture, to write in newspapers, and to edit a magazine for women. Perhaps the solution of the problem of poverty would also solve that of unpopular art and of the cakes and wine of the unpopular artist. I cannot easily understand the extraordinary position that, I am told, *The Soul of Man* has taken in the literature of revolution. It does, it is true, say many just things of the poor, as for example, its rebuke of thrift: "Man should not be ready to show that he can live like a badly fed animal." It upholds agitators. It praises the ingratitude of those to whom is given only a little of what is their own. But the essay as a whole is scarcely at all concerned with popular revolt. It is concerned less with socialism than with individualism. "The chief advantage that would result from the establishment of Socialism, is, undoubtedly, the fact that Socialism would relieve us from that sordid necessity of living for others which in the present condition of things, presses so hardly upon almost everybody. In fact, scarcely anyone at all escapes." Wilde had not escaped himself. "Under Socialism," he says, "all this will, of course, be altered." There is no need to estimate the precise quality of the irony in that " of course." If Socialism meant the ruling of the people by the people, Wilde disliked it, as a new form of an old tyranny. He took it simply as an hypothesis of free food for everybody and the abolition of property. Rich and poor alike, he supposed, were to sell all they had and give . . . to the state. He was interested solely in the development of personality, which, he thought, was hindered by the existence of private property, whether possessed or not possessed, a plus or a minus quantity. " Socialism itself," he says, "will be of value simply because it will lead to Individualism," an individualism now difficult and rare, because it consists in the free development of personality that property, plus or minus, makes almost impossible except in special cases. That seems to me to be a very different Socialism from that of the people who, accepting greedily the sops thrown to Cerberus in the course of the essay, are willing to accept the whole as a manifesto of social revolution. Wilde keeps aloof from rich and poor alike, and, throughout a long paper, more carelessly written than most of his, is simply speculating upon what art can gain by social reform, and of what kind that reform must be, if art is not to be left in a worse case than before it. The essay is like notes from half a dozen charming, and, at that time, daring talks, thrown together, and loosely brought into some sort of unity by a frail connecting thread.

In its airy distance from practical politics, nothing could be more dissimilar than *The Soul of Man* from the two letters to The Daily Chronicle. While he lived in it, Wilde had been able to disguise, at least sometimes, his lack of independence from society. When society put him in prison he was face to face with that unpleasing fact. From being the subject of ironical discussion, society and its reform became most powerful and insistent realities. The poor were no longer people whose unlovely woe he did not like to remember, but men whom he had met, men from whom he had received kindness when he, like them, was "in trouble." Reform was no longer a vague idea with possibilities at once dangerous and delightful, but concrete, and with an immediate end. It was concerned not with the development of individuality, but with saving from disaster one poor man who had disobeyed regulations in giving a biscuit to a starving child, and many poor men from sleeping unnecessarily in an atmosphere of decaying excreta. *The Ballad of Reading Gaol* was poetry and propaganda; the two letters scarcely troubled about anything but their urgent purpose, though Wilde was incapable of writing sentences that should not be dignified and urbane. A beggar had been allowed into the Palace of Art, and would not be denied.

. . . . . .

After staying in Naples for three or four months, Wilde went to Paris. In February 1898, the ballad, that he had not been able to sell to a newspaper, was published as a book. In March The Daily Chronicle printed the second of the letters on prison abuses. He wrote nothing else after he left prison, but revised *The Importance of Being Earnest* and *An Ideal Husband* for publication, and supervised the French translation of the ballad made by M. Davray, who, as he pointed out, had not had the advantage of imprisonment, and was consequently puzzled to find equivalents to some of the words. He suggested the plot of a play that another man wrote. There was talk of his adapting a French play for the English stage; but nothing came of it. He complained that he found it "not easy to recapture the artistic mood of detachment from the activity of life." He often left Paris. In December, 1898, he went to Napoule, and in the following spring to Switzerland.

His work was done, and, after the writing of the ballad, he was impotent of any sustained effort, whether in life or in literature. He lost, however, little of his intellectual activity, and none of his power of enjoyment. When he was in Rome in the spring of 1900, he learnt how to use a photographic camera, and took innumerable photographs with a most childlike enthusiasm. He was blessed by the Pope, not once only but seven times. His pleasure in watching the ceremonies of the Church recalled the year when, as an Oxford undergraduate, he had half-hoped, half-feared to find salvation, or, at least, a religious experience.

In May he returned to Paris, where his life cannot but have been humiliating to one who had been "le Roi de la vie." Many doors were closed to him and others he was too proud to enter. He spent days and nights in cafés, drank too much, and wasted his conversation on students who treated him without respect. He had sufficient money, but his extravagances often left him penniless. M. Stuart Merrill has a note from him asking for a very little sum, "afin de finir ma semaine." He was not starving, as has been suggested, nor was he entirely deserted by his friends, though most of the French writers ignored in misfortune the man they had worshipped in success. M. Paul Fort, almost the only French poet of whom in his last illness Wilde spoke with affection, spent much time with him, and remembers him not outwardly unhappy, less capable than he had been of concealing his depths, and interested in everything, like a child. Another Frenchman who saw him during these months thought him dazed, like a man who has had a blow on the head. The two opinions are not contradictory. They represent a man whose power of will has been suddenly taken from him. Wilde no longer picked and chose; he no longer, a critic in life as in art, directed his doings with intention and self-knowledge. He could no longer dominate life and twist her to the patterns he desired, but was become flotsam in a stream now obviously much stronger than himself. He could smile as he drifted, but he could not stop.

As the year went on, he fell ill, and though he rallied more than once, and never lost the brilliance and clarity of his intellect except in delirium, he grew steadily worse. His death was hurried by his inability to give up the drinking to which he had become accustomed. It was directly due to meningitis. For some months he had increasingly painful headaches. On October 10, he underwent a small operation unconnected with his illness. He rallied after the operation, and, a fortnight later, was in a condition to talk with wit and charm, as, for example, when he said that he was dying beyond his means. On October 29, he got up and went to a café. On the 30th, he was less well, though he drove in the Bois. Throughout November he grew steadily weaker, and was often hysterical and delirious. Specialists were called in consultation but could do little more than label the manner of his death. On November 29, a priest, brought by Mr. Robert Ross, baptized him into the Catholic Church, and administered extreme unction.

The following account of his last hours is taken from a letter written by Mr. Ross to a friend, ten days after Wilde's death. Mr. Reginald Turner had nursed Wilde for some time before his death, and, with Mr. Ross and the proprietor of the hotel,[1] was present when he died.

"About five-thirty in the morning (November 30) a complete change came over him, the lines of the face altered, and I believe what is called the death-rattle began, but I had never heard anything like it before, it sounded like the horrible turning of a crank, and it never ceased until the end. His eyes did not respond to the light test any longer. Foam and blood came continually from his mouth. . . . From one o'clock we did not leave the room, the painful noise from the throat became louder and louder. (We) destroyed letters to keep ourselves from breaking down. The two nurses were out and the

[1] Hôtel d'Alsace, 13 rue des Beaux Arts.

proprietor of the hotel had come up to take their place; at 1.45 the time of his breathing altered. I went to the bedside and held his hand, his pulse began to flutter. He heaved a deep sigh, the only natural one I had heard since I arrived, the limbs seemed to stretch involuntarily, the breathing became fainter, he passed at ten minutes to two exactly."

On December 3, 1900, Oscar Wilde was buried in the Cemetery of Bagneux. On July 20, 1909, his remains were moved to Père Lachaise.

# XI

## AFTERTHOUGHT

WILDE has been dead for nearly a dozen years. Already the more swiftly fading colours of his work are vanishing; already critics who fix their eyes on that departing brilliance are helping his books into the neglect that often precedes and invariably follows popularity. His life is already midway between fact and legend, between realism and glamour. His life and his books alternately illumine and obscure each other. The mutilated *De Profundis* is given a biographical importance that it does not, in its present state, possess, and the scarlet and drab contrasts of his tattered tapestry of existence blind the eyes of people who would otherwise read his books.

. . . . . . .

There is a word, often applied to Wilde in his lifetime, that has, since his death, been used to justify a careless neglect of his work. That word is "pose." In all such popular characterizations there is hidden a distorted morsel of truth. Such a morsel of truth is hidden here. We need not examine the dull envy of brilliance, the envy felt by timid persons of a man who dared to display the hopes and the intentions that were making holiday within him, the envy that used that word as a reproach, and sought to veil the fact that it was a confession. But we shall do well to discover what it was beside that envy that made the word applicable to Wilde.

Wilde "posed" as an æsthete. He was an æsthete. He "posed" as brilliant. He was brilliant. He "posed" as cultured. He was cultured. The quality in him to which that word was applied was not pretence, though that was willingly suggested, but display. Wilde let people see, as soon as he could, and in any way that was possible, who and what he was or wished to be. No bushel hid his lamp. He arranged it where it could best be seen, and beat drums before it to summon the spectators. He had every quality of a charlatan, except one: the inability to keep his promises. Wilde promised nothing that he could not perform. But, because he promised so loudly, he earned the scorn of those whom charlatans do not outwit. He has even met with the scorn of charlatans, who cannot understand why he made so much noise when he really could do what he promised.

The noise and the display that were inseparable from any stage of Wilde's career, and were not without an indirect echo and repetition in his books, were partly due to the self-consciousness that was among his most valuable assets. He knew himself, and he knew his worth, and, conscious of an intellectual pre-eminence over most of his fellows, assumed its recognition, and was in a hurry to bring the facts level with his assumption. He had, more than most men, a dramatic conception of himself. "There is a fatality," says the painter of Dorian Gray, "about all physical and intellectual distinction, the sort of fatality that seems to dog the faltering steps of kings. It is better not to be different from one's fellows." Wilde was always profoundly conscious of his own "physical and intellectual distinction," not with the almost scornful consciousness of Poe, but with a deprecating pride and a sense of what was due to it from himself and from others. Wilde's "pose"—call it what you will—is easily adopted by talent since Wilde created it with genius. Its origin was a sense of the possession of genius, of being distinct from the rest of the world. Poe emphasized this distinction by looking at people from a distance. Wilde emphasized it by charming them, with a kind of desperate generosity. He knew that he had largesse to scatter, and not till the end of his life did he begin to feel that he had wasted it, that in him a vivid personality had passed through the world and was not leaving behind it a worthy memorial. This was not the common regret at having been unable to accomplish things. It was a regret at leaving insufficient proof of a power of accomplishment that he did not doubt, but had never exerted to the uttermost. In thinking of the virtuosity of Wilde's manner, a thing not at all common in English literature, we must remember the consciousness of power that wrapped his days in a bright light, served him sometimes as a mantle of invisibility, and made him loved and hated with equal vehemence. His tasks were always too easy for him. He never strained for achievement, and nothing requires more generosity to forgive than success without effort.

This consciousness of his power excused in him an extravagance that in a lesser man would have been laughable. He would have it recognized at all costs, for confirmation's sake. He needed admiration at once, from the world, from England, from London, from any small company in which he happened to be. The same desires whose gratification earned him the epithet "poseur," made him expend in conversation energies that would have multiplied many times the volume if not the value of his writings. He pawned much of himself to the moment, and was never able to redeem it.

He leaves three things behind him, a legend, his conversation, and his works. The legend will be that of a beautiful boy, so gifted that all things were possible to him, so brilliant that in middle age men still thought him young, stepping through imaginary fields of lilies and poisonous irises, and finding the flowers turned suddenly to dung, and his feet caught in a quagmire not only poisonous but ugly. It will include the less intimate horror of a further punishment, an imprisonment without the glamour of murder, as with Wainewright, or that of burglary, as with Deacon Brodie, but a hideous publication to the world of the sordid transformation of those imagined flowers. The lives of Villon and of a few saints can alone show such swift passage from opulence to wretchedness, from ease to danger, from the world to a cell. We are not here concerned to blame or palliate the deeds that made this catastrophe possible, but only to remark that to Wilde himself, in comparison with the life of his intellect, they probably seemed infinitely unimportant and insignificant. The life of the thinker is in thought, of the artist in art. He feels it almost unfair that mere actions should be forced into a position where they have power over his destiny. As time goes on, the legend will, no doubt, be modified. It is too dramatic to be easily forgotten.

In earlier chapters I have spoken of the conversational quality of Wilde's prose, but not, so far, of his conversation, which, to some of those who knew him best, seemed more valuable than the echo of it in his

P

books. It varied at different periods and in different companies. More than one writer has described it, and the descriptions do not agree. With an audience that he thought stupid he was startling, said extravagant things and asked impossible questions. With another, he would trace an idea through history, filling out the facts he needed for his argument with bright pageants of colour, like the paragraphs of *Intentions*. At one dinner-table he discoursed; at another he told stories. Wilde "ne causait pas; il contait," says M. Gide. He spoke in parables, and, as he was an artist, he made more of the parables than of their meanings. An idea of this fairy-tale talk may be gathered from his *Poems in Prose*. These things, among the most wonderful that Wilde wrote, are said to be less beautiful in their elaborate form than as he told them over the dinner-table, suggested by the talk that passed. They are certainly a little heavy with gold and precious stones. They are wistful, like princesses in fairy-tales who look out on the world from under their crowns, when other children toss their hair in the wind. But we may well fail to imagine the conversation in which such anecdotes could have a part, not as excrescences but one in texture with the rest. No other English talker has talked in this style, and the Queen Scheherazada did not surpass it when she talked to save her life. Beside Lamb's stuttered jests, Hazlitt's incisions, Coleridge's billowy eloquence, Wilde's tapestried speech must be set among the regrettable things of which time has carelessly deprived us. I have heard it said that Wilde talked for effect. The peacock spreads his tail in burning blue and gold against the emerald lawn, and as Whistler made a room of it, so Wilde made conversation. He talked less to say than to make, and his manner is suggested by his own description of the talk of Lord Henry Wotton in *The Picture of Dorian Gray*:—

"He played with the idea, and grew wilful; tossed it into the air and transformed it; let it escape and recaptured it; made it iridescent with fancy, and winged it with paradox. The praise of folly, as he went on, soared into a philosophy, and Philosophy herself became young, and catching the mad music of Pleasure, wearing, one might fancy, her wine-stained robe and wreath of ivy, danced like a

Bacchante over the hills of life, and mocked the slow Silenus for being sober. Facts fled before her like frightened forest things. Her white feet trod the huge press at which wise Omar sits, till the seething grape-juice rose round her bare limbs in waves of purple bubbles, or crawled in red foam over the vat's black, dripping, sloping sides. It was an extraordinary improvisation."

Wilde improvised like that. A metaphor would suddenly grow more important in his eyes than the idea that had called it into being. The idea would vanish in the picture; the picture would elaborate itself and become story, and then, dissolving like a pattern in a kaleidoscope, turn to idea again, and allow him to continue on his way. Wilde talked tapestries, as he wrote them. He saw his conversation, and made other men see it. They thought him a magician.

And now that mouth is closed, from which, as from Alain Chartier's, "so many golden words have proceeded." Death has given the kiss of the Lady Anne of Brittany, and the glittering words are blown away, or fallen in the pages of other men's books to gild a meagre ground. In fifty years' time the last of those who heard him speak will be old men and dull of memory, or garrulous with tedious invention. The talk is gone. Wilde had no Boswell. All that largesse of genius has been carried away and spent, or thrown away and forgotten. A talker is like an actor. It is only possible to say, he was wonderful on such an evening, or on such another, and, as time goes on and this becomes matter of hearsay, why, it is as if his achievement had never been. For the flowers of his talk bloom only in dead men's memories, and have been buried with their skulls.

Wilde's talk is gone, but its effects remain in the conversational ease of his prose, and in the mental attitude that his writings perpetuate. The talker is, almost of necessity, a dilettante, a man who delights in, but is not the slave of, his subject of the moment. The existence of the dilettante is changeful and playful, resembling the bee-like, sweet-seeking pilgrimage of the critic, but quite distinct from it. Conversation fosters criticism and dilettantism alike, and these are Wilde's most noticeable characteristics. I have already insisted, perhaps too often, on the critical attitude of his work. He insisted on it himself. Much in his poetry and in his tales is imitative criticism, his dialogues are critical, the subject of the best of them is "the critic as artist," and he did not call *Dorian Gray* a story, but "an essay on decorative art." I have not insisted on the dilettantism that made even his multiform criticism a by-product rather than the object of his life, and allowed it to look for applause, and to reflect his conversation instead of letting his conversation borrow from its less fleeting radiance. Wilde's work is distinguished from the greatest in this: it is not overheard.

Wilde provides us with the rare spectacle of a man most of whose powers are those of a spectator, a connoisseur, a man for whom pictures are painted and books written, the perfect collaborator for whom the artist hopes in his heart; the spectacle of such a man, delighting in the delicacies of life no less than in those of art, and yet able to turn the pleasures of the dilettante and the amateur into the motives of the artist. In some ages, when talk has been more highly valued than in ours, he would have been ready to let his criticism die in the air: he would have been content that all who knew him should credit him with the power of doing wonderful things if he chose, and with the preference of touching with the tips of his fingers the baked and painted figurine over the modelling of it in cold and sticky clay. Such credit is not to be had in our time, and he had to take the clay in his fingers and prove his mastery. Besides, he had not the money that would have let him live at ease among blue china, books wonderfully bound, and men and women as strange as the moods it would have pleased him to induce. If he had been rich, I think it possible that he would have been a des Esseintes or a Dorian Gray, and left nothing but a legend and a poem or two, and a few curiosities of luxury to find their way into the sale-rooms.

Wilde preserved, even in those of his writings that cost him most dearly, a feeling of recreation. His books are those of a wonderfully gifted and accomplished man who is an author only in his moments of leisure. Only one comparison is possible, and that is with Horace Walpole; but Wilde's was infinitely the richer intellect. Walpole is weighted by his distinction. Wilde wears his like a flower.

Walpole is without breadth, or depth, and equals only as a gossip Wilde's enchanting freedom as a juggler with ideas. Wilde was indolent and knew it. Indolence was, perhaps, the only sin that stared him in the face as he lay dying, for it was the only one that he had committed with a bad conscience. It had lessened his achievement, and left its marks on what he had done. Even in his best work he is sometimes ready to secure an effect too easily. "Meredith is a prose Browning, and so is Browning," may be regarded as an example of such effects. Much of his work fails; much of it has faded, but *Intentions, The Sphinx, The Ballad of Reading Gaol, Salomé, The Importance of Being Earnest,* one or two of the fairy tales, and *De Profundis,* are surely enough with which to challenge the attention of posterity.

These things were the toys of a critical spirit, of a critic as artist, of a crtic who took up first one and then another form of art, and played with it almost idly, one and then another form of thought, and gave it wings for the pleasure of seeing it in the light; of a man of action with the eyes of a child; of a man of contemplation curious of all the secrets of life, not only of those that serve an end; of a virtuoso with a distaste for the obvious and a delight in disguising subtlety behind a mask of the very obvious that he disliked. His love for the delicate and the rare brought him into the power of things that are vulgar and coarse. His attempt to weave his life as a tapestry clothed him in a soiled and unbeautiful reality. Even this he was able to subdue. *Nihil tetigit quod non ornavit.* He touched nothing that he did not decorate. He touched nothing that he did not turn into a decoration.

I do not care to prophesy which in particular of these decorations, of these friezes and tapestries of vision and thought, will enjoy that prolongation of life, insignificant in the eternal progress of time, which, for us, seems immortality. Art is, perhaps, our only method of putting off death's victory, but what does it matter to us if the books that feed the intellectual life of our generation are stones to the next and manna to the generation after that? Of this, at least, we may be sure: whether remembered or no, the works that move us now will have an echo that cannot be denied them, unheard but still disturbing, or, perhaps, carefully listened for and picked out, among the myriad roaring of posterity along the furthest and least imaginable corridors of time.

(3988) **Oscar Wilde.**—Is there any published record available of the Oscar Wilde court trials?—J. M. B., Beyrout.
["Oscar Wilde: Three Times Tried," verbatim reports (Palmer, 63s.).]

THE END